assimil KIDS & TEENS

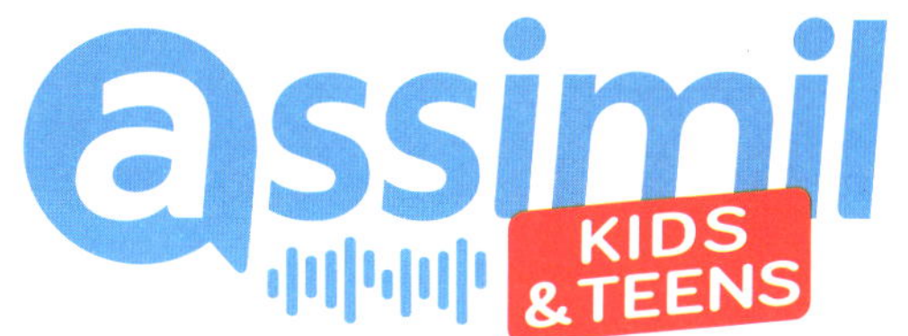

English

Nolwena Monnier • Ève Grosset

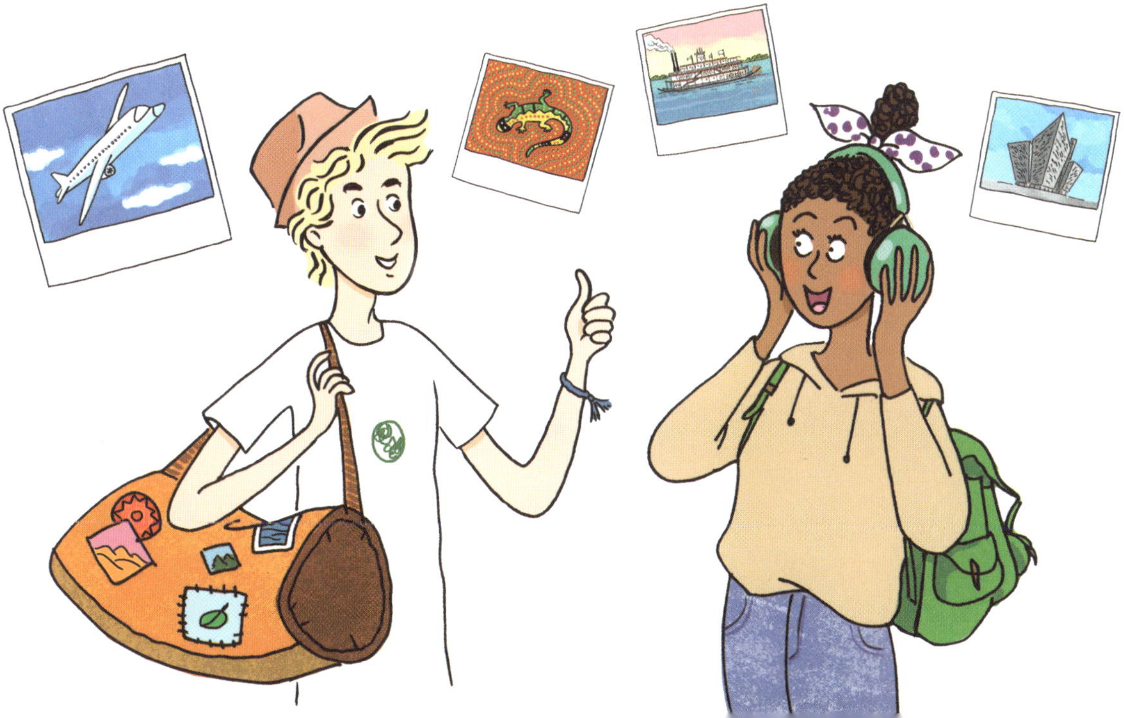

Editorial concept and graphical design: Okidokid - www.okidokid.fr

A New **Hope!**

Marc: We are so lucky, Lucie!

Lucie: Wow! I'm so happy, Marc!

M: We were right to **take part in** this competition!

L: And lucky to win it! It's just incredible!

M: This contest was super.

L: And what a prize!

M: **Can** you imagine? We **will** tour the **English-speaking world**?

L: How many countries **will** we visit?

M: I don't know. We should receive our programme soon.

L: That's so exciting! We **will** meet so many new people . . .

M: Yes! Australians, Americans, Scots **and so on**.

L: And travel to so many places . . .

M: Edinburgh, Brisbane, Washington . . .

L: We **will** taste new **kinds** of food.

M: Hamburgers!

L: You eat hamburgers every day!

M: True!

L: And we **will** visit historical monuments.

M: I dream of being **at the top** of the Statue of Liberty in New York!

L: We **will** walk around large cities and discover national parks.

M: And we **will** listen to new types of music and discover new sorts of art.

L: Wow! **It will be** exhausting . . .

M: What do you mean? Don't you want to go anymore?

L: Well, you know . . . **We will be** far from our families.

M: Lucie!

L: We **won't see** our friends for months.

M: Lucie!

L: We **will miss** class!

M: You're kidding me!

L: Yes I am! I would never give up **such a** wonderful project!

M: And I love the idea of the blog.

L: Yes! Writing about our trip is a great idea! We **can post** texts and pictures.

M: And **you can put** some of your paintings up too.

L: Oh yes! I could upload my watercolours!

M: We**'ll share the highlights** of our trip with our readers!

L: It **will be** great fun!

M: **You bet!**

L: Well, the hardest part is yet to come!

M: What do you mean?

L: Packing our suitcases!

M: Oh my . . . When are we leaving?

L: In a month.

M: Let's begin right now! I need at least a month to pack all my stuff!

READY TO SPEAK?

Answer the following questions. Make full sentences.
Did you ever win a contest? • What was it? • What did you win?
How did you feel? • Would you like to tour the world? • Why?
Which countries would you like to visit?

TOOL BOX

VOCABULARY AND EXPRESSIONS

take part in = to be involved in an activity

English-speaking world = English-speaking countries

and so on . . . = etc. **kinds** = types = sorts **at the top** ≠ at the bottom

You bet! = You're right! **highlights** = the best parts

GRAMMAR

Exclamatory sentences:

- **Structure 1 => It is such + (article) + adjective + noun(s) + !**
  She is such a lovely girl!/They are such lovely girls!
- **Structure 2 => What + (article) + adjective + noun(s) + !**
  What a wonderful dress!/What wonderful dresses!
- **Structure 3 => How + adjective + this or these + noun(s) + is/are + !**
  How incredible this book is!/How incredible these books are!
- **Structure 4 => This + noun + is/are + so + adjective + !**
  This house is so big!/These houses are so big!

TOOL BOX

will (no plural form) => express a future action

Structure => subject + will + verb Negative form => will not or won't

I **will not** go to the supermarket. I have got too much work.

They **won't** like this movie. It's too romantic.

can (no plural form) => talking about abilities

Structure => subject + can + verb Negative form => cannot or can't

I **cannot** cook today./I **can't** sing that high.

Hi everyone! Welcome to our blog!

My name is Marc, I am 18 years old and I am from Germany. This is Lucie. She is 19 and she is French. We **met last year** when we **take part in** a summer camp in Egypt. **We love** discover**ing** new cultures, meet**ing** new people and learn**ing** new languages. **Last month**, we entered in a contest to win a world tour of English-speaking countries. And we **won**!

You **will follow** our trip week after week! In each country, **we will meet** new people and discover new cultures. We **will post** pictures of monuments and tell you about our impressions about the country. You **will learn** so many fun things with us. Lucie **will** also **post** some of her watercolour paintings! She is really talented!

Do you **like** read**ing** about funny facts? Do you **love** try**ing** out new sports and activities? Do you **enjoy** watch**ing** videos of new places? Do you **hate** be**ing** bored? This is exactly what you **will find** on our blog! So **stay tuned**!

Marc

VOCABULARY AND EXPRESSIONS

last year/last month = the past year/the past month

Stay tuned! = Follow us!

GRAMMAR

Expressing a finished action in the past

=> preterite/simple past

- **Structure for regular verbs: verb + "-ed"**
  carry => carried
  stop => stopped
- **Irregular verbs => learn them by heart**
- **Auxiliaries**
  BE => I was   you were   she/he/it was   we/you/they were
  DO => did   **HAVE** => had
- **Negative form => did not/didn't + verb**

Expressing taste => like/enjoy/love/prefer/hate + verb -ing (or noun)

DID YOU KNOW?

- English is the official language in more than 50 countries around the world.
- The USA is the third most visited country in the world. The United Kingdom is the seventh one.
- Sydney Opera House is the most visited the most famous building in Australia.

You are now ready to practise your grammar! Open your exercise book at **page 3**.

Road **Trip**

Lucie: Marc! There's something in my **inbox**.

Marc: **What is it**?

L: Our programme!!!

M: Great! Let's open it!

L: OK. **How many** countries will we visit?

M: A lot!
We'll **begin by visiting** African countries.

L: **When** do we leave?

M: We'll leave **on Friday**, February 16th.

L: Wonderful! **In February**, we should have nice weather! Let me see . . . **First**, we will visit Nigeria, **second**, South Africa and **finally** Kenya.

M: **Then**, Adelaide!

L: **Who** is Adelaide?

M: Adelaide! The city in Australia . . .

L: Oh . . . OK . . . **So** we will fly to Australia?

M: Yes, **then**, Cairns and Tasmania. We must **watch out for** the Tasmanian devil.

L: I love wild animals!

M: I know! **Where will we go** next?

L: New Zealand! Auckland, Matamata and Wellington!

M: Mn-ma-matamata what???

L: They shot many movies there . . . *Lord of the Rings,* for example!

M: Great! That's my brother**'s** favourite movie! He will be really jealous.

L: We'll need to take a lot of pictures to show him.

M: OK! Let's see . . . We will **then** land in the US:
Portland on the West coast, the Midwest and **eventually** Louisiana!

L: We'll listen to jazz in the French Quarter of New Orleans!
I'll teach you to dance!

M: Oh my God . . . Where is that? Nunavut???

L: Oh, that's in North Canada.

M: **How do you know** about that?

L: Ah-ah! You know I love Native American art.
Then Ottawa and New Brunswick **but** not Quebec.

M: **How many** kilometres **will** that **be**?

L: I don't know. Too many!

M: OK! Time to go back to Europe. You will like that!

L: **Why?**

M: Ireland!

L: Yes! I love Irish music!

M: We will stay in Cork, **pop over to** Tralee for some surfing and **then** on to Galway.

L: We will visit Northern Ireland and see the Giant's causeway,
an amazing natural site.

M: Our next stop will be . . . the Isle of Man? I don't even know where it is . . .

L: Between Ireland and the United Kingdom. We'll take a boat.

M: Oh no! I get seasick . . .

L: You'll have to be brave! We'll take a boat to Wales next.

M: Wow! **What** a trip! So many kilometres . . .

L: Well, no. You should say "so many miles"!
Don't forget they use miles in English-speaking countries.

READY TO SPEAK?

Tell us about your next trip (in your country or abroad).
Where will you go? • What will you do?
Who will you meet? • What will you visit?

TOOL BOX

VOCABULARY AND EXPRESSIONS

inbox => for emails

letter box => for paper letters

begin by + verb -ing

watch out for + noun

eventually => does not mean "maybe" but "finally"

on + day => on Monday

in + month => in June

in + year => in 1515

pop over to = go to some place for a short time

GRAMMAR

Interrogative structure => **What/where/who/when/why/how + auxiliary + subject + verb + ?**

What is it? => asking about an object.

Where is it? => asking about a place.

Who is it? => asking about a person.

When is it? => asking about a moment in time.

Why are you doing that? => asking about the reason
How will we go there? => asking about the way/the manner

Linking words to organise your paragraph

=> first/second, then/finally, so (consequence), but (contrast)

Possessive case:

of with an object => The colour of this car is beautiful.
's ith a person => My mother's car is red.

Good morning guys!

We received our programme this morning! This will be **the most incredible** and **longest** trip of our lives. Our first stop will be Nigeria in Africa. I can't wait to discover Africa.

During our world trip, we will visit twenty-one different places. Can you imagine? **Among** all these destinations, I think my favourite place will be Cairns in Australia. I can't wait to discover the Great Barrier Reef. I'm fond of nature. I want to do scuba diving and watch exotic fish. I also want to see Kenya with all those wild animals. We could also learn some Bantu there. I think Lucie's favourite place will be Nunavut. She wants to meet Native American artists. She is **less attracted** by cooking or singing.

What will be YOUR favourite destination? The Midwest with its fantastic wild landscapes? Or maybe Ireland with its Celtic legends, or Wales with **its millions of sheep**? One place will be **as interesting as** the other. We'll do everything we can to make you discover **the best** of each place!

Marc

VOCABULARY AND EXPRESSIONS

can't wait to + verb/can't wait for + noun + to + verb = being very excited about something

I can't wait to eat this chocolate cake.

I can't wait for that new movie to be released.

among = amongst = in the middle of a group

Millions of sheep => no "s" on sheep, even if there are hundreds/millions of them

GRAMMAR

Comparing one thing with another

- **Superlative** = highest degree of comparison =>
  Most + long adjective: This is the most important thing to remember.
  Short adjective + -est: This is the biggest town in the country.
- **Expressing equality** =>
  As + adjective (long or short) + as: He is as intelligent as his brother.
- **Comparative of inferiority** =>
  Less + adjective (long or short) + than: This house is less cosy than the other one.

DID YOU KNOW?

- Johannesburg in South Africa is the most visited city in Africa.
- The Great Barrier Reef comprises about 900 islands.
- There are about 65,000 Inuit people in Canada.

You are now ready to practise your grammar! Open your exercise book at **page 4**.

EPISODE 03

What Does It Take to Tour the World?

Lucie: Marc, oh my God! What happened? **Somebody** broke into your house! Did they steal **anything**?

Marc: No. I'm just **packing** my **bags**.

L: Do you always take **this** many things?

M: No. I **often take** less but I never **travel** for very long.

L: Well . . . We'll leave **soon**. You should pack **now**! Will you be ready **on** time?

M: Of course! When you do thing **slowly**, you do things **properly**!

L: Yeah. I know: *chi va piano va sano* . . .

M: I did not know you could speak Italian.

L: Ah ah ah! Is **this** your **bag**? And all **these** things are supposed to go inside?

M: Don't worry! I'm **really** organised!

L: **Really**?

M: Of course! My clothes are **on** my bed, my books are **under** my desk and my toiletries are **in** the bathroom.

L: Did you make a list? You always **forget something** when you pack.

M: I won't forget **anything**!

L: **Somebody** told me you're not that organised!

M: Who???

L: Your brother! Will you take your mobile phone?

M: Of course! Why?

L: Because it is **on** the floor, **behind** the door.

M: Drat! Thanks. **Actually**, I was wondering where it was.

L: Good! You've got everything then? What about your passport?

M: My passport? Well, it must be here **somewhere** . . .

L: Well, it could be **anywhere** in **this** mess!

M: It must be in my desk. Can you have a look?

L: Sure. Here it is!

M: Phew! No time to get another one before **leaving**.

L: No time to do **anything** before leaving. Are you ready? The taxi is here, **waiting** to take us to the airport.

M: What??? Taxi? Airport? Are we not **leaving** tomorrow?

L: Yes, we are. I just wanted to see your face!

M: That's not funny. Is your **bag** ready?

L: Sure! It's **next to** my bed. I made a list some days ago and I packed yesterday.

M: Oh my God! You're so organised! That's a girl thing!

L: Don't be stupid. I **know** a lot of boys who are organised!
Your brother, for example!

READY TO SPEAK?

What do you put in your suitcase when you travel?
Are you organised?
Do you pack several days in advance?

VOCABULARY AND EXPRESSIONS

bag = piece of luggage = suitcase
travel (noun) = trip
travel (verb) = to make a trip
journey = the movement from one place to another
(The journey from London to Singapore was very tiring.)

GRAMMAR

Simple present => **habitual actions**

Subject + verb + object + complement: I walk my dog every morning.

Adverbs => **adjective + ly:** gently, slowly, quickly

Common time adverbs: always, often, never, soon, now

Demonstrative pronouns

This + singular noun: This flower (in my hand) smells so nice!

These + plural noun: These children (here) are very clever.

Prepositions of place => on, under, in, behind, next to

Verb -ing => **at the beginning of sentences or after a preposition (except "to")**

Eating fruit is good for your health.

I look forward to seeing you.

I am interested in buying this car.

Something/somebody/somewhere => **affirmative sentences**

I went somewhere very nice on holiday.

Anything/anybody/anywhere => **negative and interrogative sentences**

Did anybody know he wanted to join us?

Do you want anything to eat?

Nothing/nobody/nowhere => **negative sentences.**

Note that the verb is affirmative.

I did absolutely nothing yesterday. It was Sunday!

That's it folks!

All **my** stuff is packed. **My** suitcases are ready!

Marc has also prepared **his** bag. He has put so many things in it! **Our** suitcases are quite heavy in fact but we are leaving for a long time. We took **our** passports of course but also **my** camera. I need it to upload pictures to **our** blog regularly.

My little sister wanted to give me **her** favourite teddy bear but I refused. I know she needs it. She loves **its** nice soft fur and she sleeps with it every night. I think it was so nice of her. Could **your** sister do that kind of thing? Marc and I took one **lucky charm** each. I took **my** favourite **eraser**. It's in the shape of Italy. I bought it some years ago when I went to Milan. Marc took **his** German key ring with the colours of his home country flag. He can look at it when he feels **homesick**! I hope I won't feel **homesick** too! Get ready! **Our** blog will take off soon. First stop: Nigeria!

Lucie

VOCABULARY AND EXPRESSIONS

folks (US) = people
cuddly toy = a soft, warm toy children take to bed with them
lucky charm = an object you like a lot and you think brings you luck
eraser = an object to erase a mistake written with a pencil
homesick = sad because you are far from your country and family

GRAMMAR

Personal pronouns

Subject	Object (+ singular or plural)
I	my
you	your
he	his
she	her
it	its
we	our
you	your
they	their

DID YOU KNOW?

- More than 80,000 suitcases are lost every day in airports and railway stations.
- If you really want to tour the whole world, you will need to visit more than 190 countries.
- Most children need their **cuddly toys** until the age of six. Some keep them until age ten or twelve, others until they are in their twenties – or for the rest of their lives!

You are now ready to practise your grammar! Open your exercise book at **page 6**.

Connected Cocoa

Lucie: I'm so glad to be in Nigeria.

Marc: Me too. And so happy to meet Dunjuma.

Dunjuma: Lucie? Marc?

L: Yes! You must be Dunjuma.

D: Yes, I am. Welcome to my father's plantation.

M: Your cocoa trees are so nice.

D: Thanks.

L: Can you tell us about yourself, Dunjuma?

D: Sure. I'm 18 years old. My father **has owned** this plantation **for** 20 years. I **have worked** with him for 4 years.

M: Do you like working with your father?

D: Yes, of course! It is a family business, you know.

L: What do you do on the plantation?

D: Well, my father takes care of the trees and I take care of selling our products. We **have exported** our cocoa to Europe **for** many years.

M: So you grow cocoa beans and you export them.

D: Yes. We also have banana trees. We must diversify if we want to succeed!

L: That must be hard work.

D: It was, yes, but it **has improved** a lot **since** I was young.

L: Really?

D: Yes. We'**ve used** the Internet for years now.

M: You use the Internet?

D: Of course! Look. I **have downloaded** different apps on my mobile phone.

M: Really?

D: Yes. For example, one shows when the cocoa beans are ready for **harvest**.

L: Fantastic!

D: I can also check the price of cocoa on the international market.

L: Wow!

D: Look! I **have planned** my work with this app for three years.

M: **Wicked**! You're so connected!

D: If you say so! Wait for me here! I'm going to pick up the electric car to show you around.

L: Electric car?

D: Yes! We are **eco-friendly** here, you know!

M: Oh my . . .

L: What's wrong?

M: Well I'm trying to upload pictures to our blog . . .

L: And?

M: I can't! I have no Internet connection . . .

READY TO SPEAK?

Answer the following questions using full sentences.
Have you used the Internet for a long time?
Do you like spending time on the Internet?
What do you use it for? • Social media? • Looking for information?

VOCABULARY AND EXPRESSIONS

harvest = the period when you pick fruit or vegetables
wicked = normally: horrible, bad
In the dialogue: fantastic, incredible
eco-friendly = good for the planet
environmentally-friendly = good for the environment
user-friendly = easy to use
a pet-friendly = open to pets and their owners (for example: a pet-friendly hotel)

GRAMMAR

Present perfect

- **Structure => have/has + past participle (verb +ed or irregular verbs)**
  She has watched TV for 5 hours!
  Have you spoken with my mother recently? No, I haven't seen her for weeks.
- **Use => the action started in the past and continues to the present**
  I have watched television for hours today.

TOOL BOX

- **For + length of time** (indicate how many hours/days/weeks/months/years)
  I have lived in New York for 5 years.
  He has waited for him for many hours.
- **Since + starting point of an action**
  => since + subject + verb (past-tense form)
  I have loved this actor since he started acting.
  => since + day/month/year
  We have worked here since February.

Here we are in Nigeria.

What a wonderful country! It **has been** one of the most populated countries of Africa **for** years. You can find oil but also cocoa and banana trees. It is the rainy season at the moment but it is still hot! It **has been** like that **for** weeks. Believe me, there are a LOT of mosquitoes and they just LOVE me!

We met Dunjuma. He is just like us! He **likes protecting** nature and is a connected young man! We visited his father's plantation with him. He **has taken** care of it **for** 4 years. We saw cocoa and banana trees. He also has a few mango trees. We tasted **the best mangoes ever**! Marc ate two kilos of them and . . . was sick, of course!

We also visited the drying house. That is the place where the cocoa beans dry. This step is necessary before workers can put the beans in big bags. Trucks transport the big bags to Lagos. Abuja is the capital but Lagos is the biggest city in the country. This is where the harbour is. Then, men put the bags on large boats and cocoa is exported to Europe. **Thanks to** Nigeria, we can celebrate Christmas and Easter with excellent dark or milk chocolate!

Lucie

VOCABULARY AND EXPRESSIONS

Thanks to = because of

Thanks to my tourist guide, I knew which places to visit.

Because of this awful headache I had yesterday, I could not go to work.

GRAMMAR

Like + verb -ing => I like reading books and watching TV.

Structure => The + best + noun + ever

The best mangoes ever = We have never eaten such good mangoes before.

DID YOU KNOW?

- There are 27 other languages in Nigeria apart from the official languages: English, Hausa, Yoruba and Igbo.
- There are 8 national parks with wild animals in Nigeria.
- Nigeria has tall, modern buildings and traditional mud-wall houses.

You are now ready to practise your grammar! Open your exercise book at **page 11**.

South Africa **Past and Future**

Nelson: Are you Lucie and Marc?

Lucie: Yes. I'm Lucie. You must be Nelson.

N: Yes. Nice to meet you.

Marc: Nice to meet you too and thank you for being our guide today.

N: I'm very happy to show you **a little** part of Cape Town in South Africa.

L: Where are we going?

N: Bo-Kaap.

M: Sorry?

N: Bo-Kaap. It means "on the edge of Cape Town".

L: Is that where you live?

N: No, but I have friends there. Here we are!

L: Oh my God. It's beautiful!

M: Yes! It's so colourful.

N: I know! That building there is the Bo-Kaap museum.

M: It's a large house.

N: In fact, the Dutch built it to house African slaves **a few centuries ago**.

L: Oh my God! That's horrible.

N: I know. People decided to paint their houses in bright colours only **a few years ago** to celebrate their Muslim identity.

M: I know so **little** about your country.

N: Well . . . Slaves came from a few countries in Africa such as Mozambique or Madagascar.

L: **Did they** all **live** in Bo-Kaap?

N: No, there wasn't enough housing. The people who live here now are descendants of Indian, Sri Lankan and Indonesian families who arrived in Africa more than **300 years ago**.

M: Do you know a lot about these families?

N: No. We have **little information** about them. Where they came from, how many they were exactly. . .

L: Is it a protected area?

N: Now, yes. It had little protection **a few years ago** but now, it is a **National Heritage Site**.

M: Good! The architecture is stunning.

L: All those colours! They will make wonderful pictures for our blog.

M: You should take a picture of this brown one.

N: Brown one?

M: And also of these dark pink houses.

N: Dark pink? But . . .

L: I will also take a picture of this one. I love its light pink colour.

N: Hey! Hold on! Are you sure you're OK?

L: Of course, Nelson. We just want pictures for our blog.

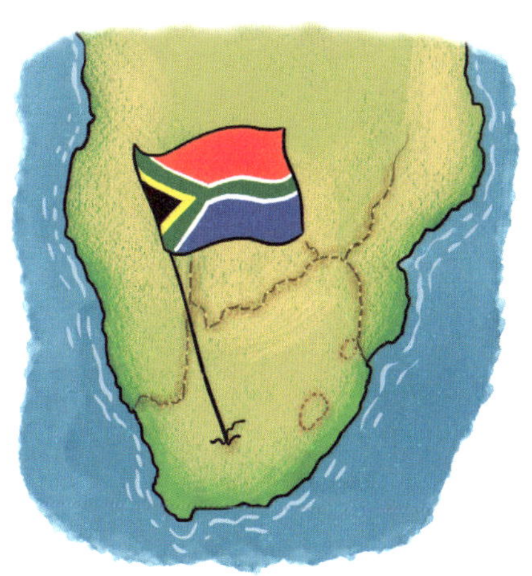

N: I know that but . . . There are no brown, dark or light pink houses in this street. They are green, orange and yellow.

M: Oh sorry, Nelson. It's just Lucie! She is **colour-blind**!

READY TO SPEAK?

Do you like visiting cities? • Why or why not?
What type of activities do you like to do when you travel?
Visiting places? • Playing sports? • Reading or doing nothing?

TOOL BOX

VOCABULARY AND EXPRESSIONS

National Heritage Site = a place protected for its historical, natural or artistic/architectural value and interest.
colour-blind person = someone who sees colours differently from other people.

GRAMMAR

Expressing something in the past

Subject + preterite + time + ago =>
My parents bought our house 5 years ago.
I went to the swimming pool some weeks ago.
Negative form => subject + did not/didn't + verb + time + ago
My parents did not buy our house 5 years ago.
I didn't go to the swimming pool some weeks ago.
Questions => when + did + subject + verb + complement?
When did you buy your house?/When did you go to the swimming pool?

Expressing a small quantity of something

A few => people or things you can count

A few people came to the concert.

A little => people or things you cannot count or money

There's a little soda in my glass.

I have only a little time before I leave.

A few/a little = some

Few/little => same structure but means that there is a small quantity of something

There were few cakes on the table (and a lot of children wanted one).

He gave us little information (so we could not understand everything).

Good afternoon everyone!

I hope you're doing fine. Did you have a look at the new pictures I posted? Yesterday was just great! We visited Bo-Kaap, a historical part of Cape Town, the second most populated city in South Africa. That's the place where slaves lived. The houses are all painted in bright colours. Marc tried to make Nelson believe I'm colour-blind. But **he** is, not me!!! Naughty him! We also loved the museum, which was really moving. It's a place **full of** history.

Today, Nelson took us to the Cape of Good Hope. We **could** see the famous African Penguins. There were so funny! But we **could** also see ostriches. They were more than **two metres tall**. We **could** also watch whales. They often come not very **far from** the shore. It's **gorgeous**!

These two days were amazing. One was historical and urban and the other one was natural and wild. South Africa is full of contrasts. **It is a pity** a large part of the population still lives in townships. And maybe you guessed but . . . Nelson got his name from . . . Nelson Mandela. With the end of Apartheid in the 1990s, Nelson Mandela became the first black president of South Africa after many years in prison. Our friend Nelson may want to become president one day . . . Who knows?

Lucie

TOOL BOX

VOCABULARY AND EXPRESSIONS

full of = containing a lot of things in/not empty
two metres tall = a person or animal measuring two metres in height
far from = not close to
gorgeous = very beautiful
It is a pity => to express regret

GRAMMAR

Expressing a possibility in the past

Structure => subject + could + verb + complement

She could go to the museum yesterday.
They could see the stars last night.

DID YOU KNOW?

- In South Africa, about 80% of the population is black, 9% is white, 8% is mixed-race and 2% is Indian or Asian.
- There are 11 official languages in South Africa.
- 4% of the world's population is colour-blind, mainly men.

You are now ready to practise your grammar! Open your exercise book at **page 12**.

EPISODE 06

A Full-Time Job

Marc: Look at Kilimanjaro!

Lucie: It's incredible. It's so high!

M: For sure! It's almost 6,000 meters high!

L: Is there always snow at the top?

Kofi: Yes! Well, **global warming** is increasing but the situation is still OK. In the 1990s, it rained so much that the reserve became a real **swamp**.

M: Hi. You must be Kofi?

K: Yes. I'm Ranger Kofi.

L: Hi, Ranger Kofi. Thanks for meeting us!

K: I'm always happy to meet young people and talk about my job.

M: **How long have** you **worked** in the Amboseli National Park?

K: I **have worked** here **for** 8 years. I **was** 20 years old when I started.

L: You **were** very young!

K: I **finished** high school and **wanted** to find a job.

M: And you **looked** for one in the national park?

K: I **have** always **loved** animals. It is essential to protect them!

M: When **did** the park **open**?

K: It opened in 1940. It **has been** a National Reserve **since** 1974.

L: Wow! It's **been** a long time! I **thought** it **was** more recent!

M: And how many animals are there?

K: It's hard to know because they are free to run where they want! There are about 1,000 elephants and 20 lions.

L: Can they live peacefully?

K: Well . . . There are illegal hunters and **poachers** who are looking for elephants in the park to kill and steal their ivory.

M: That's disgusting!

K: That's why we are here! We chase them and arrest them when we can.

M: Do you catch a lot of them?

K: They often hunt at night so it is more difficult for us . . .

L: How many rangers are there in the park?

K: Not enough! And we cannot put cameras in the park to keep an eye on the elephants! We would need thousands of them to cover the whole area.

M: Can we see the elephants?

K: Yes, of course. I'll bring the car! See you in a minute.

L: Wow! That will be great! Do you have your camera?

M: Of course! You're not the only one who takes good pictures!

L: Marc?

M: Yes. What?

L: I don't think you'll be able to take any pictures . . .

M: Why not?

L: Because! You **forgot** your battery at the hotel . . .
An elephant would not have forgotten!

M: I definitely do not have the memory of an elephant . . .

READY TO SPEAK?

Do you like wild animals? • Do you often go to the zoo?
Have you ever been to a national park in a foreign country?
Do you prefer dogs or cats?

VOCABULARY AND EXPRESSIONS

global warming = a gradual increase in the Earth's temperature that modifies the climate
swamp = very wet area/a place with a lot of water
poachers = people practising illegal hunting

EPISODE 06

TOOL BOX

GRAMMAR

Preterite VS present perfect

- **Preterite => expresses the action in the past**

I bought a book yesterday. => It happened yesterday, it is a finished action.
I lived in London three years ago. => Now I live somewhere else.

- **Present perfect => expresses an action which began in the past but is stll affects the present**

Subject + have/has + past participle (-ed or irregular) + complement
I have walked my dog every day this week. => I began walking two hours ago and I still do while I'm speaking.
She has taken pictures of this village since we arrived.

- **Negative form => have not/haven't or has not/hasn't**

I have not walked my dog every day this week.
She hasn't taken pictures of this village since we arrived.

- **Asking questions: for how long/since when**

How long have you lived in this house? I have lived here for 3 years.
Since when have you lived in this house? I have lived here since I moved to the city.

What a day!

We **visited** the national park with Kofi as our guide. Right **in front of** us, there **were** elephants, lions but also zebras, gnus, hippopotamuses **and** even giraffes.

In the evening, Kofi **took** us to a Maasai village to visit his aunt. He **was** born **in** Nairobi, the capital of Kenya, but part of his family lives **in** the Rift area. We walked **across** the village. After, we **had** dinner with the chief of the village and his family. Sitting **behind** the villagers, we could listen to traditional African stories. **Behind** us, we **heard** a lion roaring **but** nobody **was** scared. Lions don't come **into** villages.

We **stayed outside** for part of the night. **Above** our heads, a **starlit sky** and **around** us everything **was** silent. **Beside** us, there were teenagers just like us. **At** the beginning, they **looked** us **up and down but** quickly, we **realised** that we **had** a lot **in** common: the protection of wild animals, Global Warming but also our future jobs, our friends, our families, our love affairs. We all share the same joys and worries wherever we live in the world!

Marc

VOCABULARY AND EXPRESSIONS

in front of = on my opposite side/facing/ahead

but => expresses contrast

in + city/in + country => In Paris, in France

across = over/all around

TOOL BOX

VOCABULARY AND EXPRESSIONS

behind = opposite of "in front of"
outside = not inside
above = overhead
around = surrounding something or someone
beside = close to/next to
up and down = from head to toe
starlit sky = a sky full of stars

GRAMMAR

Telling a story **=> you can use the simple present, also called narrative present, or preterite as in the blog to recount past events.**
The dog comes in and starts barking./We stayed outside for part of the night.

DID YOU KNOW?

- There are more than 300 national parks in Africa.
- Maasai people practise a traditional jumping dance called *adumu*.
- The name Kenya comes from *Kiinyaa*, which refers to the highest mountain in the country. It means "mountain of the ostrich" as there are so many of these animals living in the area.

You are now ready to practise your grammar! Open your exercise book at **page 13**.

Native **Art**

Marc: Wow! The Adelaide Festival of Arts is great.

Lucie: Australian people are so creative!

M: Yes! I loved the ballet we saw yesterday **even though** it was a bit . . . strange.

L: I loved it! It was so . . . different!

M: Different, yes . . . **Let's have a look** at this art gallery. I think there's native art exhibited.

Amelia: Good morning. I'm Amelia. **May I help you**?

M: Hi. We are looking for native art.

A: **If** you**'re interested in** native art, I have something in the other room. Come with me.

L: Wow! I love these paintings!

A: They are called Dreamtime paintings **because** they represent the origin of the world, the Dreamtime.

M: Amazing! This is all very symbolic!

A: Indeed. **Consequently**, they represent natural elements such as rivers and mountains but also animals.

L: I think what I like most are the colours.

A: **In order to** mix them, artists work with natural pigments. **However**, you can find paintings with chemical pigments **but** we don't exhibit that type of work.

M: Do you mean that some artists use industrial pigments **instead of** creating their own?

A: Exactly! That's what we call fake native artists!

L: How can you see if the pigments are industrial ones?

A: **Unless** you visit the artists' studios, you can't. **As long as** you trust your artists, there is no problem.

M: Do you have smaller paintings? I'd like to take one back home but these big paintings won't fit in my bag!

A: Yes. We have some small reproductions. This way, please.

L: The Adelaide Festival of Arts is wonderful.

A: True. It is a real **asset** for all kinds of artists.

M: I hear that more and more people come every year.

A: Yes! **That is the reason** why this festival has run for so long. The mix of arts is genuine and exciting.

L: Would you have a place to recommend?

A: Sure! You should go to the Parklands.
There is an outdoor exhibit of different sculptures.

M: **Thanks for the tip**!

A: Will you stay for the whole festival?

L: Unfortunately, no. We need to go to Cairns. We are meeting someone who protects coral but I will always remember what you said about native art. It was very moving.

A: I hope these Dreamtime paintings will give you sweet dreams.

M: Don't worry. We won't let the bedbugs bite!

READY TO SPEAK?

Do you like art? • Why? • Why not?
What type of events do you go to?
Do you often visit art exhibits?
Have you ever been to a concert?

VOCABULARY AND EXPRESSIONS

Let's have a look = Why don't we go and visit?
May I help you? = polite offer of assistance
to be interested in: She's interested in art.
asset = strong point = advantage
Thanks for the tip. = Thank you for this idea/piece of advice.

TOOL BOX

GRAMMAR

Expressing contrast

even though = although

Even though he is an excellent swimmer, he lost the race.

although = whereas = however = nevertheless

Although it was raining, we went for a walk.

It was raining in the city whereas it was dry in the country.

It was raining. However, we went for a walk.

It was raining. Nevertheless, we went for a walk.

But: I like spinach but I prefer carrots!

Expressing opposition

On the contrary = on the opposite

You don't like my dress, right? No, no! On the contrary, I love it!

Expressing an objective

In order to: In order to succeed, you must work more.

Expressing consequence

Consequently = Thus = Therefore

He behaved badly. Consequently/thus/therefore, he was punished.

Expressing a length of time

As long as + subject + verb

You can stay with me as long as you like.

Expressing replacement/possibilities

Instead of + verb -ing

Instead of looking for her keys, she sat down on the sofa.

Unless + subject + verb

Unless you ask them, you will never know what happened.

TOOL BOX

Expressing causes

Because + subject + verb

Because it rained, we did not go outside.

Because of + (determiner) + (adjective) + noun

Because of the heavy rain, we did not go outside.

This is the reason why/this is why

He was so late! This is (the reason) why I was so upset.

The Adelaide Festival of Arts is just incredible!

We went to concerts and plays, exhibitions and ballets. We also watched some good movies! We had great fun! I love the connection to nature: using symbols like rivers or mountains and painting with natural colours and materials is just great!

When we visited the Parklands we met a group of young people. They study at the Adelaide School of Art. **They told us about** Australian art. One of them, called Barry, is a native Australian. He told us that, **at first**, Aborigines were oppressed by Western settlers. The situation has improved **but** they are still discriminated against. It is **therefore** it is important to recognise their specific form of art.

They also took us to the beach. **Even thought** the weather was not very nice, we spent the evening sitting on the sand **while** watching the sun going down **into** the sea in front of us. Behind us, there were the tall buildings of the city. We could hear the noise of traffic from far away and the noise of the waves a lot closer. One of Barry's friends took his guitar and they all sang Australian traditional songs. We went to bed very late that night but it was a **once-in-a-lifetime** evening!

Lucie

VOCABULARY AND EXPRESSIONS

to tell someone about + noun/pronoun = to discuss something
once-in-a-lifetime = an opportunity that won't be possible again, something you live only once
into = in + to

GRAMMAR

Linking words

at first = first = in the beginning
even thought + subject = despite the fact that => contrast
thus = therefore, for this reason => consequence
while + subject + verb/while + verb -ing = at the same moment
While (I was) waiting, I saw a fire engine rushing.

DID YOU KNOW?

- Adelaide is the 5th most populated city in Australia, after Sydney, Melbourne, Brisbane and Perth and has a larger population than the capital city, Canberra.
- It is the only city which accepted British men during the 19th century. All the other cities only welcomed prisoners who were sent to settle in Australia.
- Queen Adelaide gave her name to the city in 1836 when Australia was still a British colony.

You are now ready to practise your grammar! Open your exercise book at **page 17**.

OK **Coral!**

Marc: Wow ! What a view! The colour of the ocean is amazing!
Somewhere between green and blue.

Lucie: Look! There's a young man over there. That must be Archie. Archie?

Archie: Hi! You must be Lucie and Marc.

M: Yes! Thank you for welcoming us to Cairns.

A: The most beautiful part of Australia!

L: What's your job exactly?

A: I'm a **volunteer** for the AFR, the Australian Foundation for Reefs.

M: And what is your **aim**?

A: Well . . . We **want to save** the coral. The Great Barrier Reef is so fragile . . .

M: And I suppose global warming doesn't help?

A: Of course not! We **don't want the coral to die**.
People sometimes think that the corals are stone but they are not, they're really alive.

L: What do you do precisely?

A: We have **volunteers** who visit schools.
We **want children to participate** in our campaign.

L: They must be your best ambassadors!

A: Yes, they are! It's great when you see them so involved.

L: So you **want Australians to preserve** their natural habitat.

A: Exactly! We **want volunteers to help us**. They can give money to the foundation, of course, but also help us clean the beaches or inform people about the problem.

M: What is your best memory as a **volunteer**?

A: I remember when I attended the Earth Forum we organised last year with other **charities**.

L: Why?

A: I remember the children's faces when I told them about the 7th continent! They were so shocked!

M: The 7th continent? What is that?

A: A continent **made of** plastic! **Made of** pollution in fact!

M: What???

A: It's a large area made up of plastic bags, plastic bottles **and so on**. It represents several tons of **garbage**.

L: Wow. And where is it?

A: In the Pacific Ocean.

L: Oh my God!

A: I know! That's why the children were so shocked!

M: I bet they were!

A: And as a result, they cleaned a **nearby** beach with their teacher.

L: They **wanted adults to understand** that we all must act.

A: Yes! They promised to do it every year!

L: You must be proud of them!

A: Yep! That's what I like about volunteering!

M: Well . . . It takes time and energy but it's so rewarding!

A: I bet it does! Are you ready for scuba diving?

M: Sure! Let's meet some fish and observe the Great Barrier Reef!

L: I hope there won't be too much rubbish in my pictures!

READY TO SPEAK?

Do you like visiting aquariums?
Do you think it is important to protect marine flora and fauna?
What do you think of plastic pollution in the sea?

VOCABULARY AND EXPRESSIONS

volunteer = someone who works for free, often for a charity
aim = goal = objective
charity = several people who join to defend a cause (poverty, health, nature, etc.)
and so on = etc.
garbage (US) = rubbish (UK) = waste
nearby = close, not far
made of = material used to make something (made of steel, made of wool,...)

GRAMMAR

Expressing someone's will/what he or she wants

- **To want to do something => want + to + verb + complement**

  I want to go on holiday!

  She wanted to buy a new manga!

- **To want someone to do something => want + noun/pronoun + to + verb + complement**

  You want your children to clean the car.

  They wanted their teacher to explain the lesson again.

- **Negative form => want + noun/pronoun + not + to + verb + complement**

  He wants his dog not to jump in the lake.

  He didn't want his dog to jump in the lake.

Meeting Archie was great!

He **could have talked** for hours about corals. It was the first time I went scuba diving. I was **a bit** scared but Archie was a very good teacher. We were able to watch multicoloured **fish** and even a turtle.

On the following day, he took us to the countryside. There are **huge** farms in Australia with lots of cattle and several hundred animals. They can also grow fruit. **Sometimes** you must still drive off-road for dozens of kilometres to reach the farms in the **Outback**. Everything is so big here!

A lot of young **foreigners** work on the farms. They can earn a bit of money and learn English. It is also the opportunity for them to meet people from all around the world.

They usually only stay for what is called a **"gap year"**. They told us it is a hard work, very tiring but the atmosphere is great and they learn a lot during their stay. We **should have done** that too!

We **would have liked** to stay longer with them but we took the plane for another destination! Talk to you soon!

Marc

TOOL BOX

VOCABULARY AND EXPRESSIONS

a bit = a little
huge = very very big/enormous
cattle = a group of animals (cows, sheep, etc.)
sometimes = not all the time
Outback = wild and arid area in the centre of Australia
one fish/two fish (no 's'). He caught two fish.
foreigners = people who are not from the same country
⚠ **strangers** = people you don't know but who do not necessarily come from another country
gap year = a year before going to university during which you travel, act as a volunteer, learn a foreign language, etc.

GRAMMAR

Could, would, or should?

- **Could + have + past participle** => something was possible in the past but was not done
  You could have walked faster. You could have been on time!
- **Would + have + past participle** => something was possible in the past but not anymore
  I would have earned more money with another job!
- **Should + have + past participle** => something did not happen and you regret it
  We should have cleaned the car before going on holiday.

DID YOU KNOW?

- The Great Barrier Reef is more than 2,600 kilometres long.
- The coral becomes white and dies when the sea water turns too hot.
- Immigrants came to Cairns in the 19th century to work in the gold mines.

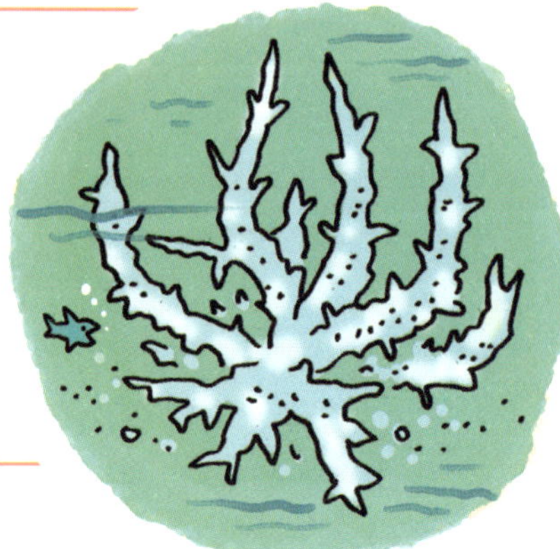

You are now ready to practise your grammar! Open your exercise book at **page 18**.

Weird Animals!

Marc: I did not even know about Tasmania before we landed!

Lucie: It's a small island compared with Australia but it has a strong identity.

Paula: And unique **native animals**! You must be Marc and Lucie?

L: And you must be Paula?

P: Yes! Welcome to the University of Tasmania.

M: **Thanks for welcoming** us.

P: Well . . . I was really impressed by your project. Visiting all these English-speaking countries must be exciting.

L: Yes! And meeting new people is, too!

P: I will introduce you to new people. You'll see. Come this way!

M: Do we **need to walk** for long?

P: Yes. We'll go to another part of the uni.

L: Hold on! I **need my camera**!

P: I think you will. This way, please.

M: Wow! What are they?

P: Wombats. They are marsupials, like kangaroos.

L: Wow. I knew we were supposed to see marsupials but I didn't think they would be so close. What do they eat?

P: They are herbivores. They eat grass and roots.

M: Look **over there**!

P: Those are Tasmanian devils.

L: Ouch! Devils?

P: Yes. They are called that because of their bark that scares people to death.

M: They smell really bad! Their house **needs cleaning**.

P: That's their smell when they're afraid.

L: Do we scare them?

P: Well. They **need a quiet environment**. They don't often have visitors in this part of the campus!

M: They are quite impressive with their long teeth.

P: True. Come this way. I want you to meet the thylacines, also called wolf or tiger of Tasmania.

M: Where are they?

P: Here, on this screen. Watch! This animal was officially declared extinct in 1986.

M: Oh no . . .

P: You know, wombats and Tasmanian devils are also protected. They **need protection** now more than ever.

M: Wow. There're so many **endangered species** . . .

P: I know. At the University of Tasmania, we **need to study** them to better protect them.

M: Your work is great.

P: Thanks. By the way, where is your friend Lucie?

M: She's almost certainly taking pictures of wombats and Tasmanian devils. We **need to put** some on our blog.

P: Oh. Here she comes. What's wrong?

L: Well . . . The wombats just disappeared in the high grass and the Tasmanian devils barked at me so loudly that I ran away!

P: You know, Lucie, they are wild animals!

L: Yeah but they could be wild and nice! Marc is wild sometimes but always nice! Maybe I will put a picture of him on the blog then.

READY TO SPEAK?

Do you like taking pictures? • What do you take pictures of? Your family and friends? • Landscapes during your holidays? Pictures of sporting activities?

VOCABULARY AND EXPRESSIONS

native animals = endemic = animals or plants which live in a specific geographical area

thanks + for + verb -ing = Thanks for helping me.

over there = in that direction

endangered species = animals which must be protected because they are in danger

TOOL BOX

GRAMMAR

Need => something which is essential, that you must have/do

Different structures:

- **Need + noun**: I need a new school bag!
- **Need + verb -ing (passive meaning)**: This house needs fixing, especially the roof.
- **Need + to + verb** => same meaning as "must": You need to practise your German. = You must practise your German.
  You need to watch this movie. It's great!
  = You must watch this movie. It's great!

Morning everyone!

Discovering all these typical animals **from** Tasmania was incredible. Paula was a fantastic guide. **Last year**, she **took part** in a boat race **from** Sydney **to** Hobart to collect money for the protection of animals. She is a good sailor. Her husband prefers cars. He has been going to Targa Tasmania, a car rally, **for several years** now.

Do you want to hear some fun facts about school? In Tasmania, students **go to** class from Monday to Friday and school **finishes** as early as 3 p.m. They **have** assemblies. That's when all the students **gather** to share common information . . . And what's funny is that they **have** their summer holidays in December and January. That's because they are in the southern hemisphere so their summer is during our winter! Paula also told us they **wear** uniforms and they can choose their courses. I would give up maths if I could. You can even win an award on a special occasion, for example if you helped someone, if you participated in class or if you did well at sport during an official match! I would love to go to school in Tasmania! Mum? Dad? Would you be OK if I stayed here for a few more months?

Marc

TOOL BOX

VOCABULARY AND EXPRESSIONS

from . . . to => from starting point to end point (in space or time)

from New York to Boston from Monday to Friday

from 8 a.m. to 1 p.m. from March to June from 1914 to 1918

gather = collect, unite (transtitive), congregate (intransitive)

GRAMMAR

Simple present => **describing habits**

I take my breakfast every morning and go to school by bus.

Preterite/simple past => **talking about something in the past**

I went to Australia last year.

Present perfect => **talking about something which began in the past and is still true in the present**

I have studied Portuguese for two years.

DID YOU KNOW?

- Tasmania comprises one main island and 334 smaller ones.
- The three main islands' nicknames are *The Island of Inspiration*, *The Apple Isle* and *Holiday Isle*.
- Abel Tasman, a 17th-century Dutch explorer and navigator, discovered Tasmania. His name was given to the island in 1856.

You are now ready to practise your grammar! Open your exercise book at **page 20**.

EPISODE 10

Let's score!

Marc: Good morning. We're looking for Kasia and Ted.

Woman: Morning! They are **in** the lounge. This way.

M: Kasia? Ted? We're Lucie and Marc.

Kasia: Hi! Nice to meet you.

M: Nice to meet you too.

L: So you're rugby and cricket players?

K: Yes. I play rugby and Ted plays cricket. **Both** sports are very popular **in** New Zealand.

M: How long have you lived **in** Auckland?

K: I'm **from** Auckland in fact, so all my life.

Ted: I moved **to** Auckland one year ago to join my new cricket team.

M: And how many training sessions **a week** do you have?

T: One every day and I also spend time running.

K: Same for me. I train with my team every day. In addition, we have individual body-building training.

L: Wow! That's a lot of work.

T: Yes! We'll have a special training session **in May**, before the end of the championship.

K: Do you play sports, Lucie and Marc?

M: Well. Not that much . . .

L: Marc? The only sport he plays is video games!

M: **Come on**! You don't play sport either!

L: Yes, I do! I dance **twice a week**. Hip hop and jazz!

T: Great! I love dancing.

M: Seriously? Dancing is not a sport!

L: Well . . . If we look at your dancing . . .
That is clearly not a sport. Let's go back to you, Kasia and Ted.
Do you have matches every weekend?

K: Yes! **On** Sunday, we have a very important match for the national championship. You should come!

L: Sure! We'd love to watch you play! Do you think there will be a lot of people?

K: Actually, women's rugby is more and more popular but it has not always been easy.

M: Really? Why?

K: The first men's championships took place **in the 19th century** whereas the first Women's World Cup only took place **in** 1991.

L: Wow! More than a century later!

M: Was it the same for cricket?

T: Not really. Cricket was opened to women a lot earlier than rugby.

K: You know, sexism is still very present in some sports.

M: That's very unfair! Girls should be able to play the same sports as men.

T: And men the same sports as women!

L: Well, you know . . . It's just like how some guys don't consider dancing to be a sport! When you hear that, you know there's still a long way to go!!!

READY TO SPEAK?

Do you think girls and boys can do the same activities?
Do you like doing activities which are traditionally for girls or boys? • Do you think girls and boys can do the same jobs?

TOOL BOX

VOCABULARY AND EXPRESSIONS

both + noun => two things together

both movies are great!

a week = every week

How many books a week do you read? About five!

How many times a month do you go to the swimming pool? I go three times a month.

once = one time

twice = two times

three times, four times, etc.

Come on! = Seriously? = Are you kidding? = Really?

GRAMMAR

Prepositions

In + place => no movement => I live in Delhi.

To + place => movement => I want to go to Italy on holiday.

From + place => origin => I come from Ireland.

On + day => We went to the forest on Saturday.

In + month => I will begin learning Russian in September.

In + year => The first world war began in 1914.

In + the + number + century => The Industrial Revolution took place in the 19th century.

⚠ 1st, 21st, 31st, 41st, etc.
2nd, 22nd, 32nd, 42nd, etc.
3rd, 23rd, 33rd, 43rd, etc.

What a match!

Our friend Kasia scored 4 times! We were so proud of her. Her boyfriend Ted was there to **explain** the rugby rules **to** us! Marc did not **feel like playing**. First, he could not because it was a women's match but anyway he does not run **fast enough**!

On the following day, Ted took us to Whangaparaoa, on the North-East coast of New Zealand. (Marc still cannot pronounce this name properly!), a few kilometres away from Auckland. He **lent us bikes** and we rode them in the Gulf Harbour Marina and in the park nearby. It is a very nice place where you can also hire a boat and sail in the bay. You can also see fish. Marc knew he could not **give food to** the fish so he tried to take pictures of them and almost fell into the water!

Because I **felt like swimming**, we went to Little Manly Beach. We picked up a marvellous shell on the beach. I wanted **to take it to** my sister who collects them. We also tried stand-up paddle and we had a lot of fun! Before leaving, we had a soda and pavlova, a traditional cake from New Zealand. That was a wonderful taste of New Zealand!
Talk to you soon!

Lucie

TOOL BOX

VOCABULARY AND EXPRESSIONS

Adjective + enough/enough + noun => insufficient lack of something, an insufficient amount of something

This race was not long enough./There is not enough food on the table.

GRAMMAR

Preposition or no preposition

- **Feel + like + verb -ing** = to want to do something, to have the desire to do something

  I feel like eating chocolate.

- **Explain something to someone**

  The teacher explains the lesson to the pupils.

- **Give someone something** = give something to someone

  He gave me his biscuit./He gave his biscuit to me.

- **Bring someone something** = bring something to someone

  They will bring me some drinks for the party.

  They will bring beverages for the party to me.

- **Lend someone something** = lend something to someone

  My neighbour lent me his bike./My neighbour lent his bike to me.

DID YOU KNOW?

- The Haka performed at rugby games is a traditional Maori dance.
- Cricket and baseball are not similar! The balls, the bats and the grounds are different. The organisation is also different.
- Auckland was built around 50 extinct volcanoes.

You are now ready to practise your grammar! Open your exercise book at **page 25**.

EPISODE 11

Welcome to New Zealand!

Anahera: Lucie! Marc! We're here!

Marc: Anahera! Tamati! Nice to meet you!

Tamati: *Haere mai!*

Lucie: Sorry?

A: *Haere mai!* It means "welcome"!

M: OK! Is this Maori language?

T: Yes! We belong to the Maori language.

A: Our language is also **called** *Te Reo* which means "the language".

L: **Is** it **spoken** only in New Zealand?

T: No. The Maori people are the native people of New Zealand but you can also find Maori communities on different Pacific islands. You know, this language **is spoken by** many people.

L: Really? I thought it was quite a small community.

A: Not at all! It is true that the language almost disappeared in the past.

T: That's because the Pacific islands **were colonised by** different Western countries.

L: So English became the predominant language?

A: Exactly but Maori language **has been taught** in primary schools for several years now. You can even study Maori language and culture at university. The writing system **was set up by missionaries** in the 19th century so it uses the Latin alphabet, like English.

M: That's great! Does Maori culture have other specificities?

T: Yes. We have tattoos!

A: Men and women have tattoos in Polynesia. They are part of our life!

M: I love those! And I would love to have one!

A: You can't. They are very symbolic. You must belong to a Maori community.

M: Too bad. What about the Haka! We see it on TV at every rugby match!

A: Yes! That's certainly the best known aspect of Maori culture.

T: The dance is made for scaring people before fighting.

M: Wow! Anahera, what are those people doing over there?

A: Oh. They're preparing Hangi.

L: Hangi? What is that?

T: Hangi is a way to prepare food. First, a hole **is dug** in the ground, and then **embers are put** into it.

A: After, you put a little bit of **soil** on the **embers** and you can cook your meat and vegetables in a sort of bag with herbs.

L: That must be good!

T: It is delicious.

M: Can we taste some when it's ready?

T: Sure! How long are you staying?

L: I don't know. Why?

A: Because it takes at least 4 hours to cook!

M: Wow! It takes longer that *pot au feu* or *eisbein*!

T: What are those?

M: Traditional French and German dishes!

READY TO SPEAK?

Do you speak a regional language? • At home? • At school?
Would you like to learn one? • Why? • Why not?

VOCABULARY AND EXPRESSIONS

missionaries = priests, people sent on a religious mission. Some of them participated in colonisation.
embers = small pieces of burning or glowing wood.
soil = earth in which flowers or trees are planted.

GRAMMAR

Passive form => the subject becomes the object

Active form: subject + verb + complement =>
passive form: subject + be + past participle (+ by + agent).
The cat eats the mouse. => The mouse is eaten by the cat.

GRAMMAR

- **Present** => The Maori language is spoken by a lot of people.
- **Past** => The Maori language was spoken by a lot of people.
- **Present perfect** => The Maori language has been spoken for decades.

⚠ This example uses a combination of two different past participles: the first correponds to the present perfect structure (have/has + past participle) and the second corresponds to the passive form.

The Maori language has been spoken for decades.

Been => past participle of "to be"

Spoken => past participle of "to speak", used to form the passive

Spending time with Anahera and Tamati was really nice!

They are passionate about their culture! After, Marc and I wanted to meet a teacher at Massey University, Prof. Longworth. He told us about his research projects about the Maori culture at the university. Here is his interview:

"Maori culture **must be taught** at university. It is really part of New Zealand culture and history. This **should be implemented** by a real educational **policy**. This course **could be taken** by Maori people but also by students with occidental origins. It would be an opportunity for them to learn more about the Maori culture. In our projects, we explore different aspects of that culture: the language of course but also Maori identity **through** art and literature. People **would be puzzled** by how rich this culture is. Maori culture was certainly influenced by Western culture but, in turn, it has influenced the culture of

New Zealand." Meeting Prof. Longworth was great, especially when he showed us an automatic translator! We were magically able to speak Maori. And of course . . . Marc tried some swear words!

Lucie

TOOL BOX

VOCABULARY AND EXPRESSIONS

policy = a political measure
through = thanks to

GRAMMAR

Passive with modals

Modal + be + past participle

This **must be taken** into account before making a decision!
It **could be considered** to be true!
This book **should be translated** into Maori.
This act **can be taken** as an example of kindness.
Teachers **would be surprised** by his efforts.

DID YOU KNOW?

- Since 1987, the Maori language has been one of the national languages of New Zealand together with English and NZ Sign Language.
- Tattoos are very popular in Maori culture. They have a lot of different symbolic meanings.
- Do you like kumara? Kumara is a sweet potato used in Maori cuisine.

You are now ready to practise your grammar! Open your exercise book at **page 26**.

EPISODE 12

Lord of **the Cinema!**

Lucie: Happy birthday to you . . .
Happy birthday to you . . .

Marc: Oh! Thank you, Lucie.
I love strawberry cupcakes!

L: They're the only type of cake I could easily bring!

M: You know . . . I'm so glad I can celebrate my birthday here!

L: I **knew** that it **would** be your favourite place!

M: Matamata . . . What does that mean?

L: Well . . . The **women** at the entrance gate said it comes from a special kind of turtle.

M: OK . . .

L: There must be some on the beaches nearby . . .

M: I guess . . . Can you imagine how many famous **people** have been here?

L: And now, you!

M: Visiting the Hobbit village was just one of my dreams!
I'm such a big fan of *Lord of the Rings* movies.

L: You're like a **child**!

M: All **children** love magic!

L: I **know** you**'re** a big child! No, I'm kidding! You're right! Matamata is just magic!

M: This is the trip of a **life**time!

L: Yeah, we will remember this place our whole **lives**!

M: I looked for **information** about it.

L: Really? And what did you find?

M: Do you know how many movies have been shot here?

L: No . . . How many?

M: A lot!

L: Wow! That's a **piece of information**!

M: Don't make fun of me! It's my birthday!

L: That's right! It's your day!

M: I heard on the **news** that new movies are going to be shot here!

L: That's not surprising. The cinema industry is pretty developed in New Zealand.

M: They have such wonderful landscapes!

L: True. And great actors and filmmakers.

M: Having all those technicians, makeup artists and facilities here must be quite amazing.

L: It's also a good **way** to bring money to the area!

M: Oh please! It's not only a money matter! It's art! Creativity! Magic!

L: You're so enthusiastic!

M: Cinema is such a trendy art!

L: Hum . . . Marc? You know what is not trendy? Can I give you **a piece of advice**?

M: Of course! As **much advice** as you want!

L: Close your mouth! You've got pieces of cake between in your teeth!

TOOL BOX

READY TO SPEAK?

Have you ever seen a movie being filmed? • Have you ever participated in one? • Would you like to? • Why? • Why not?

VOCABULARY AND EXPRESSIONS

Irregular plurals

man => **men** cameraman => **cameramen**

woman => **women** spokeswoman => **spokeswomen**

one person => **several people** (people can be singular but with another meaning)

one child => several **children**

one life => several **lives**

irregular plurals in "-a": = phenomenon => **phenomena**

criterion => **criteria** medium => **media**

information, advice, furniture => uncountable nouns, no "s", to specify there is only one => use "a piece of"

The information is important.

This is a good piece of advice.

Much advice is given in this book.

news, means => uncountable nouns, always a "s", to specify there is only one => use "much" and not "many"

The news is incredible.

I don't have much money.

GRAMMAR

Sequence of tenses

When there are two parts to your sentence (principal clause and relative clause), you should use tenses carefully!

- **simple present/will** => subject + simple present + (complement)/subject + will + verb + (complement) = I know very well you won't eat spinach.
- **simple past/would** => subject + simple past + (complement)/subject + would + verb + (complement) = I guessed he would arrive late.

The area of Matamata is just wonderful!

When you look down, the countryside is blossoming. You can see **fish** in lakes and rivers but there are also **sheep**, **calves**, **geese** and **deer** in the fields and forests. Maybe there are also even **wolves**! I just hope there're not mice! I'm too scared of them! In March, the **leaves** turn orange and red as winter is beginning. The colours are amazing and the countryside incredible. Nature is quiet . . . well . . . as long as there aren't **masses** of people! I hate touristy areas and I hate noisy areas too!

The sea is never very far in New Zealand. We went to Tauranga, a few kilometres from Matamata. The beach was great but we decided to eat first. Lucie wanted to try a typical dish from New Zealand and . . . did not like it at all! She didn't want people to see so we left the restaurant as soon as we had paid! I liked walking in the park. We ate ice cream and this time, Lucie was happy! **Come** and **visit**! **Enjoy** and **make** the most of it! Matamata is more than just the magical Hobbit village!

Marc

TOOL BOX

VOCABULARY AND EXPRESSIONS

Irregular plurals:

foot => **feet** goose => **geese**
wolf => **wolves** leaf => **leaves** calf => **calves**

- **Fish, sheep, deer => no "s"**

The word is singular or plural depending on the context.
This fish is very good./These fish are the most sustainable.
A baby sheep (a lamb) needs its mother./Sheep are usually very noisy.

- **Plural with "-es" : words ending in "ss", "x" and "ch"**

mass => **masses** box => **boxes** match => **matches**

GRAMMAR

Imperative

=> giving orders or encouraging people to do something:

Verb + (complement) Watch this!/Don't do that!

DID YOU KNOW?

- Matamata has several TV channel offices which is quite unusual for such a small town.
- Dame Catherine Tizard was born in Matamata. She was the first woman to become Mayor of Auckland (from 1983 to 1990) and also the first woman to become Governor-General of New Zealand (from 1990 to 1996).
- Hobbiton can be visited. The government decided to leave the movie set in place because it did not harm the environment.

You are now ready to practise your grammar! Open your exercise book at **page 28**.

Flea Market Day

Lucie: New continent, new activities.

Marc: Yes. I'm so glad to be in the US. Portland seems great!

L: Yes. I am so happy to visit the West Coast.

M: You know, Portland is a very green city.

L: No, I didn't know . . . Can you tell me **where we are going** now?

M: To the flea market!

L: Really! I have never been to a flea market!

M: I have. I remember going with my parents **when I was** about 12.

L: And did you like it?

M: Well . . . Not really! It was just old things to me . . . But I was only 12!

L: I'm sure you will love it now! **Second-hand** things are so nice!

M: Yes! Re-using instead of buying new things is always great.

L: Look at that **stuff**!

Woman: Hi! How are you doing?

M: Fine. Thanks.

W: Are you looking for something special?

L: Not really. Just **having a look**!

M: I was wondering **what this is**?

W: That? Oh, it's an old tool.

M: What are you supposed to do with it?

W: I have absolutely no idea **how to use** it!

L: I like the lamp just behind you . . .

W: Oh sorry . . . Somebody **who came** earlier already bought it.

L: **Never mind**! It wouldn't fit in my suitcase anyway!

W: Are you here on **vacation**?

M: Not exactly. We're touring the English-speaking countries and we also decided to write a blog.

W: That's great! Who decided to visit Portland?

L: The organisers did! They wanted us to know **why and how the city became** so green!

W: **Woo, it's been a long road**. A lot of work has been done and the city is greener than ever! Bike lanes, electric public transportation, recycling bins everywhere, positive energy buildings . . .

M: Nice! Can I see that bracelet?

W: Sure! It's made of silver.

L: I like it. How much is it?

W: $15.

M: That's cheap. I'll buy it.

W: You know, **second-hand** products are usually cheap.

L: And it's a good way to recycle things.

M: And what's that? I think I can see some interesting things . . .

W: That? Well . . . That's just the **trash** . . .

READY TO SPEAK?

Do you often go to flea markets? • Do you like them? • Why? Why not? • Do you prefer buying new or second-hand objects?

TOOL BOX

VOCABULARY AND EXPRESSIONS

second-hand things/objects = used products, not new ones
stuff (informal) = things
having a look = to have a look = looking without buying
Never mind! = it does not matter = no problem
vacation = American English word for "holiday"
trash = American English word for "rubbish"
It's been a long road! = It has taken a lot of time and effort.

GRAMMAR

Indirect questions

- **Structure => independent clause + relative clause**
  relative clause = relative pronoun + subject + verb + (complement)

I want to know what this is!/I wonder why it was so cold there.
My aunt will soon tell us where we are going.
Just tell him when he can come.
They wanted to know how this machine works.

TOOL BOX

Indirect questions

• **Structure => subject + relative clause + verb + (complement)**
relative pronoun + subject + verb + (complement)

The main clause is in orange. The relative clause is in blue.

Necessary with "who", optional with the other pronouns

⇨ **The man who is walking** his dog **is my neighbour.**

⇨ **The place where we went** on holiday **was very quiet.**

• **Structure => main clause + whose + object + subject + verb + (complement)**

I cannot tell you whose bike it is./I don't know whose book he will read.

Portland is really a green city!

We met several people along our walk in town. They told us about all the changes that have taken place over the years. The tram came first. Then they developed parks and green areas. Most people now go to work **on foot or by bike**. They **regularly** organise recycling and flea markets to encourage people to re-use things.

The city has even received different awards: 'greenest city in America' and 'second greenest city in the world'. People are very proud of this! They are so **environmentally-friendly** and the city is so well looked after! We could learn so much from them!

There is also the highest concentration of vegan restaurants in the country. I wanted to test one but Marc likes meat too much! I eventually convinced him to come and in fact ... he loved it! Everything is **locally-sourced** from farms around the city and **ecologically-transported** by bike or electric cars. **Well done** Portland!

Lucie

VOCABULARY AND EXPRESSIONS

by + means of transport => by car or by bike

on foot

GRAMMAR

Adverbs => adjective + "-ly"

Close => closely

⚠ If the adjective ends with an "l", double it for the adverb

Beautiful => beautifully

Compound adjectives => adverb + "-" + past participle

Well-done/nicely-said

DID YOU KNOW?

- The biggest flea market in the US takes place in Brimfield (Massachusetts) with more than 5,000 stands.
- Portland is surrounded by several extinct volcanoes.
- There are twelve bridges in Portland that cross the Willamette River, including five with metallic structures from the beginning of the 20th century.

You are now ready to practise your grammar! Open your exercise book at **page 32**.

EPISODE 14

The Middle of **Nowhere**

Lucie: I'**d rather be** in Chicago. We could visit all its wonderful museums . . .

Marc: Come on! Stop complaining . . . Look around you! Big open spaces. After Portland, a few outdoor activities are nice.

L: I don't like horses.

Aishling: I'm sure you'll like these!

M: Aishling? Hi. I'm Marc and this is Lucie.

L: Hi, Aishling . . . Sorry, I didn't mean to be **rude**.

A: You'**d rather** be on your sofa watching TV, right?

L: Not really. I prefer taking pictures or painting.

A: I'm sure you'll like the ride. There are some fantastic pictures to take!

M: Where are you going to take us?

A: **Up to you**! We can visit an American Indian reservation or take a ride in Roosevelt National Park.

L: The reservation!

M: I'**d rather go** to the park!

L: I'**d rather visit** the reservation!

A: Well . . . You'**d better** make up your minds!

L: OK. Let's **head for** the park.

M: No, you're right. We should go to the reservation.

A: Listen! We can go to the reservation through the park.

L: Let's do that, then!

M: Your farm seems very isolated!

A: It sure is. You need to drive 20 miles from the main road to reach the entrance.

L: Isn't it difficult living far from the city when you are 16?

A: Not really. There's a lot to do on the farm. We're busy **from dawn to dusk**.

M: So you don't really know what is happening in the world?

A: Well, we don't have TV at home.

M: What??? No TV?

A: No. You know, there's a lot more to do than watch TV!

M: Sure but . . . I mean . . .

A: We don't have a TV but we do have a home cinema, wifi internet and a connected house.

L: Isolated but connected!

A: Yep! You know, I'm only here on weekends since I go to **boarding school**.

L: So you stay the whole week at school and only come back to the farm on weekends?

A: Yes, and I prefer being outside to watching a movie, even on a large screen.

L: You bet!

A: Oh, oh . . . Get ready! Here is the American Indian reservation.

READY TO SPEAK?

What would you rather do? • Play sports?
Visit an art exhibit?
Make up at least five different sentences with "I'd rather".

TOOL BOX

VOCABULARY AND EXPRESSIONS

rude = not nice, impolite
up to you = you choose, you decide, I don't mind
head for = go in a particular direction
from dawn to dusk . . . = from sunrise to sunset/from early morning to late at night
a boarding school = a school where you stay and sleep in dormitories

GRAMMAR

Expressing preferences/giving advice

- **'d rather** (would rather) = I'd prefer + verb -ing
  Structure : subject + "would rather" + verb + (complement)
  He'd rather be at home (than at school).
- **'d better** (had better) = should + verb
  Structure : subject + "had better" + verb + (complement)
  They'd better hurry (if they want to be on time).

Yihaaaa!

Whether you like big spaces **or** not, you will be impressed by the Midwest. We had the opportunity to visit an American Indian reservation. It was amazing! Like Aishling, most teenagers study at boarding schools. It is quite usual in these isolated areas.

Then, we moved to South Dakota to see one of the strangest things on Earth. If you like **either** art **or** history, you will be impressed. Mount Rushmore presents huge sculpted portraits of four American presidents: George Washington, the first president, Thomas Jefferson, who bought Louisiana from France, Abraham Lincoln who ended slavery and Theodore Roosevelt, the youngest American president.

You feel so small looking at them from the valley. This place was made to attract tourists and it works! About **three million** people come every year. **Whether** you want to learn about American history **or** you just feel like seeing an unusual monument, you will like Mount Rushmore. Lucie could not **figure out whether** she should take pictures **or** look silently at the landscape. In fact, she did not do any of these as . . . she just fell asleep after our long walk in the mountains!

Marc

TOOL BOX

VOCABULARY AND EXPRESSIONS

figure out = to determine, to solve

three million tourists => no "s" to million when it is followed by a noun

There were millions of tourists. There were three million tourists.

There were hundreds of people. There were two hundred people at the demonstration.

GRAMMAR

Giving the choice

- **Either . . . or . . . + noun:** You can have either tea or coffee.
  Either one or the other, thanks. I don't mind.
- **Whether . . . or . . .** => + subject + verb + (complement)
  Whether you want to go to the mountains or to the sea, we can travel to the US.
  Whether you like it or not, I will do it!

DID YOU KNOW?

- In October 1871, a terrible fire destroyed a part of Chicago, where most of the houses were made of wood.
- The Midwest produces more corn every year than any other region of the world.
- There are 326 Native American reservations in the US.

You are now ready to practise your grammar! Open your exercise book at **page 34**.

A Taste of **New Orleans!**

Tom: Lucie! Marc!

Lucie: Tom! Nice to meet you!

Marc: Thanks for welcoming us to New Orleans!

L: Where are you taking us?

T: I can take you to the French Quarter to begin with!

M: **Have** you **been living** in New Orleans for long?

T: No. In fact, I moved here three years ago when I began university but I fell in love with the city.

L: What do you like most?

T: I don't really know. The architecture **for sure**, the atmosphere **as well**, and the people of course!

M: **Have** you **made** a lot of friends?

T: Yes! The residents are very friendly. Many have a different culture from yours so it's really interesting to meet new people.

L: And can you take us somewhere original?

T: Sure! I can take you to the Voodoo Museum.

M: Voodoo? Are you sure?

T: Don't be scared, Marc! People **have been practising** voodoo for ages here . . . It's tradition.

M: I don't like the idea.

L: Come on, Marc! Let's immerse ourselves in New Orleans culture! Don't worry, I'll protect you!

T: OK for the Voodoo Museum then. Marc, what do you feel like doing?

M: Well . . . I'**ve been dreaming** of listening to real jazz.

T: You're right. New Orleans is the birthplace of the most famous jazzman: Louis Armstrong! We can do that tomorrow if you want!

L: I would also love to visit a **plantation**.

T: Sure! There's one not very far from here!

L: In fact, we visited Bo-Kaap in South Africa. Slaves lived in this part of Cape Town.

T: Visiting a **plantation** will be interesting for you, then.

M: It's going to be sad visiting a **plantation**. All the people who died there . . .

L: Are you afraid of the ghosts of slaves? People say there are some on **plantations**!

T: What **have** you **been expecting** on this trip?

M: I'**ve been expecting** something really traditional. But not scary!

T: OK. Then, I know! Tonight, I'll take you to a place for gumbo!

M: Gumbo? Great! I love it!

T: Really? **Have** you ever **tried** it?

M: Never but I love dancing.

L: Dancing? Marc . . . Gumbo is a dish! It's rice and shrimp. Are you planning to dance with shrimp?

READY TO SPEAK?

What type of activities do you enjoy? • How long have you been doing them? • Give different examples like "I have been playing the piano for eight years."

VOCABULARY AND EXPRESSIONS

for sure = certainly = surely = indeed

as well = also

plantation = in the US, a farm with slaves where cotton and sugar were grown

GRAMMAR

Present perfect continuous

- **Structure : have/has + been + verb -ing**

  I have been listening to you carefully.

  She has been waiting for him for hours.

- **Present perfect** => began in the past and ends in the present.
- **Present perfect continuous** => began in the past and ends in the present with an emphasis on continuity.

  I have planted new tulip bulbs. I'm done now!

  I have been gardening all morning and I still need to plant some flowers.

Time in the French Quarter

Tom took us to the **French Quarter** in New Orleans. We **had** never **been** there before. He also told us about the **Cajuns**. They have been Americans for centuries but they were once French! Indeed, they still speak French. Well, a curious kind of French according to Tom! He also showed us the steamboats. We wanted to have a tour on the Mississippi but they **had** already **finished** their day . . . and having dinner on the boat was really too expensive for us!

On the following day, we left for a sugar plantation. We visited the main house, called "big house" as well as the slave quarter. Slaves lived there for years before they were freed. That part of the visit was very moving. It was hard to imagine people living in such bad conditions. It was very different from the movie *Gone with the Wind* I **had watched** some years ago. The only thing I remember were the large crinoline dresses. I **had wondered** at the time how women could walk and endure them in such heat!

Louisiana is full of life with music and food, but it also has a tragic history!

Lucie

TOOL BOX

VOCABULARY AND EXPRESSIONS

French Quarter = a central area of old New Orleans where the French settled in the 18th century.
Cajuns = French people who moved from New Scotland, now in Canada, in the 18th century.

GRAMMAR

Past perfect

=> used to show that an event took place before another past event

Structure => subject + had + past participle + (complement)

Mary **was** late yesterday. She **had** never **been** late before.

Bob **arrived** at the airport at 3 p.m. Before that, he **had picked up** his brother.

DID YOU KNOW?

- The nickname of the state (they all have one!) is the Pelican State because there are a lot of pelicans in the Gulf. The bird is also on the state flag.
- Louisiana was French and then Spanish, and then French again before becoming American. At that time, Louisiana was a very large state which went from the Gulf of Mexico to Canada. Nowadays, the size of former Louisiana is equivalent to 13 current American states.
- Baton Rouge is the capital city of Louisiana. Its French name comes from the translation of a Native American word.

You are now ready to practise your grammar! Open your exercise book at **page 35**.

EPISODE 16

Please **Meet . . .**

Marc: I love **hiking** in the forest!

Lucie: It's so peaceful here.
Thank you for bringing us here, Ana.

Ana: I really like this part in Nunavut.

L: Do you come here often?

A: No. I live in Winnipeg with my parents but I meet my friends here as often as I can!

M: Why did you want to bring us here, then? All I can see is . . . snow!

A: I want to show you the **aurora borealis**.

M: Wow! Wonderful! Hmm . . . Are we going to walk for long?

L: Are you tired already, Marc?

M: Well . . . No but . . . We could have rented snowmobiles.

L: They're too noisy, Marc! We wouldn't be able to enjoy this wonderful silence!

A: **If you want** to see the **Northern Lights**, **we'll have to walk** about two more hours.

M: Will we meet your friends there?

A: Yes. They are preparing the campsite.

L: Are we staying the night?

A: Yes. We can even stay for a few days. In the daytime, we can observe moose or beavers. Groundhogs may be awake too !

L: Great. **If** I see some, I'll take pictures!

M: I can hear a river . . .

A: Yes. It is down there, behind that small hill.

M: Oh . . . I want to see it . . . Maybe there is salmon to fish!

L: Come back, Marc!

A: **I would not go if I were you**!

M: Why not?

A: You might meet Big Foot.

M: Big Foot?

L: Yes. He's a kind of Yeti!

M: A Yeti? No . . .

Paul: What's wrong, Ana?

A: Oh! Hi, Paul. How are you? Don't worry, it's just Marc.

L: Ana told him that Big Foot is in the area

P: Well. I haven't seen him in a while. But there might be bears . . .

L: Marc . . . Oh my God! What happened???

M: I fell in the river . . .

L: See . . . **If you had listened** to me, **you would not have got** so . . . wet!

A: Come on guys! Only a few hours' walk and we can warm up by a nice wood fire!

L: Will there be marshmallows?

A: Of course! No campsite is complete without marshmallows! But no Big Foot, Marc. I swear!

READY TO SPEAK?

What would you do if you visited a foreign country?
Make up sentences with "If I go to . . . I will . . ."

TOOL BOX

VOCABULARY AND EXPRESSIONS

hike = walking in the forest or the mountains.
aurora borealis = **Northern Lights** = natural colourful phenomenon which occurs near the North Pole.

GRAMMAR

If . . . => Condition but quite sure it will happen
If + subject + verb (simple present) + (complement)/subject + will + verb + (complement) => If I see them, I will tell them.

- **Condition but possible**
  If + subject + verb (simple past) + (complement)/subject + would + verb + (complement) => If I had money, I would buy presents for all my friends.
- **Condition but too late**
  If + subject + verb (past perfect) + (complement)/subject + would + have + past participle + (complement) => If they had thought about it before, they would have gone somewhere else.

If I were you, I would eat more fruit!
In this sentence, you can use "were" or "was'. Both are correct but "were" is more hypothetical than "was".

A night to remember . . .

I must admit I'm not very **keen on** astronomy but that night was just magic. We saw an incredible natural phenomenon: the aurora borealis, the polar lights. The colours are fantastic. I'm **still** impressed. I don't know **yet** how to describe it! I had **never** seen anything like that.

We met Ana's friends too. Some of them live in Winnipeg like Ana and others live in the area. Their parents work in mining or forestry. Some small towns are really isolated and teenagers enjoy outdoor activities. At our age, they have **already** learnt about wild life and know how to protect themselves in the woods. It is the most isolated area I have **ever** visited.

Life is different but also quite similar to ours: teenagers go to school, play sports and have fun. They just do things differently: they go to school on snowmobiles, go ice canoeing and camp in the snow.

I'm not sure I could **get used to** this kind of life but when you are born here, I guess you cannot imagine another way of living!

Marc

VOCABULARY AND EXPRESSIONS

be keen on + noun/verb -ing = like, enjoy

get used to + noun/ verb -ing = to acquire the habit of doing something

TOOL BOX

GRAMMAR

Still => **subject + (auxiliary) + still + verb + (complement)** => Something true yesterday, today and tomorrow) => I still like playing with my dolls!

Already => **subject + (auxiliary) + already + verb + (complement)** => something done once and then another time => She has already studied that lesson.

Never => **subject + (auxiliary) + never + verb + (complement)** => Affirmative sentence with a negative meaning => They've never been to this place before.

Ever => **subject + (auxiliary) + ever + verb + (complement)**
With negative sentences or questions =>
Have you ever met Paul? Don't ever talk to me like that!

Yet => **subject + verb + (complement) + yet** => I haven't met them yet, but I will tomorrow.

Too = **also** => **subject + verb + (complement) + too** => Paul is very nice too.

DID YOU KNOW?

- Nunavut has 4 official languages: English, Inuktitut, French and Inuinnaqtun.
- There are over 634 recognized First Nations in Canada. "First Nations" is the expression used to designate Native Canadians, Canada's first inhabitants.
- The first written text on the Far North dates back to 1576 and was written by the English explorer Martin Frobisher.

You are now ready to practise your grammar! Open your exercise book at **page 40**.

EPISODE 17

What Are **You Saying?**

Helena: Marc? Lucie?

Lucie: Yes . . . You're not Peter!

H: No. I'm Helena, Peter's girlfriend.
He will wait for you at the Science Museum.

L: Oh! OK!

Marc: What did she say?

L: She said that Peter would wait for us at the Science Museum.

M: OK. Let's go then!

L: Peter works at the Science Museum, right?

H: Yes. It's his student job. He wants to become a scientist.

L: Wonderful!

M: What did she say?

L: She said Peter wants to become a scientist.

H: You will see. The museum is really nice. You will like the interactive exhibitions.

L: Sure. I'm more interested in art but Marc loves all kinds of science.

H: That's great. This way, please!

M: What did she say?

L: She said that we'll love the museum.
For God's sake, what's wrong with you, Marc?

M: Can you understand her?

L: Yes, of course! Why?

M: Well . . . She has a very strong accent, hasn't she?

L: It's a Russian accent. She must be Russian.

M: I don't know where she's from but I'm **having a hard time** understanding her!

L: Be careful **not to be rude**! She might hear you.

M: I'll try but I can't understand a word she says.

H: Peter is in charge of educational programmes. He must communicate with schools to organise day trips to the museum for little ones.

L: That must be very interesting to see students enjoying science!

H: Oh yes! It is. We need to cross the road over there.

M: What did she say?

L: **She said Peter has to deal with school visits**.

H: Here we are! Peter is waiting for us at the entrance door. Oh! Here he is, with a group of children.

Peter: Hi, everyone. I'm Peter. Nice to meet you, Lucie. Nice to meet you, Marc.

M: Hi, Peter.

P: Let's go this way. We can begin the visit with the aircraft section.

L: Oh my God . . . What did he just say?

M: **He said that we could see the old aircraft**. What's wrong, Lucie? A problem with his accent?

L: Not at all. It's just very noisy in this museum with all those kids visiting.

READY TO SPEAK?

Play with a friend or a family member.
One of you says something and the other one repeats beginning with *"You said. . ."*

VOCABULARY AND EXPRESSIONS

having a hard time = having difficulties with something/a situation

to be rude = not being nice to somebody

GRAMMAR

Indirect speech => when you want to report somebody's words

- **Examples of introductory verbs: say, declare, explain, shout, etc.**
  Nothing changes when the introductory verb is in the simple present as in the example :
  "They prefer watching horror movies." => She says they prefer watching horror movies.
- **With "I", the subject changes:**
  "I like drawing landscapes." => He/She says he/she likes drawing landscapes.
- **With an introductory verb in the simple past**
  Simple present => simple past
  "They love reading mystery novels." => I explained (that) they loved reading mystery novels.

TOOL BOX

- **Present verb -ing => past verb -ing**: "We are enjoying ourselves."
  => He thought (that) they were enjoying ourselves.
- **Will => would**: "I will come tomorrow at 3 p.m."
  => He said (that) he would come tomorrow at 3 p.m.
- **Must => had to**: "She must finish her work before noon."
  => They explained (that) she had to finish her work before noon.
- **Can => could**: "We can go to the restaurant."
  => We said (that) we could go to the restaurant.
- **Don't forget to change pronoun when necessary**: "I like my cat."
  => She said (that) she liked her cat.

Ottawa is wonderful!

Oh my . . . We had a hard time understanding people's accents here! Well, other people may think that we have an accent . . . Ottawa is a really international city. It is also the capital of Canada. I'm sure some of you thought it was Montreal, didn't you?

We loved the museum. I would have loved to be able to visit such a museum when I was a kid. The interactive exhibits were really fun. **There's a chance** to test an aircraft simulator and also dig like real archaeologists. The planetarium was also stunning! It **may** be hard to believe but Ottawa is not the most populated city in the country. Its name comes from Odawa, the name of the first tribe who lived there. In May, the Canadian tulip festival illuminates the city. It is **perhaps** the **liveliest** festival in the area.

We still have a few days to spend here. **Maybe** we're going to have snow before we leave. It's Spring, but it **might** still snow. In the winter, you can even ice-skate on lakes in the area! It's a pity we came in spring. I would have loved that!

Marc

VOCABULARY AND EXPRESSIONS

liveliest => superlative of lively = bright, energetic

GRAMMAR

Expressing possibility

- **Modal: might or may**

  (Use "may" if the situation is more likely to occur)

  Subject + modal + verb + (complement)

  We may go to pick him up at the railway station but I 'm not sure.

  They might listen to his speech if they arrive on time.

- **Adverbs: perhaps, maybe**

  Can be placed at the beginning of the sentence or in mid-position.

  I will maybe go to the hairdresser tomorrow.

  Do you know if he is supposed to come tomorrow? Perhaps . . .

- **Expressions: There is a chance that . . . There is a possibility that . . .**

DID YOU KNOW?

- In the winter, you can skate on the Rideau Canal in Ottawa.
- Ottawa is home to 14 national museums.
- Queen Victoria chose Ottawa as the capital of Canada in 1857 (Canada was a British colony at that time).

You are now ready to practise your grammar! Open your exercise book at **page 41**.

EPISODE 18

Do You Speak . . . ?

Lucie: What are we going to do today, Marc?

Marc: We're going to meet Laura and her friends.

L: Nice! Where are we meeting them?

M: At school.

L: At school?
You could have chosen somewhere else . . .

M: No. It will be great. They study in a bilingual high school here in New Brunswick.

L: Really? That must be nice. What languages do they speak?

M: English and French. In fact, in New Brunswick, **2/3** of the population speaks English and **1/3** speaks French.

L: Why is that?

M: It's historical. The place had been colonised by the French and then it was colonised by the English. Both communities still live here together.

L: OK . . . It **has been** hard for Laura to mix both languages.

M: She **said it was** hard because she could speak English very well but she had a hard time with French.

L: Oh. She's an English-speaker!

M: Yes. Her parents both come from another part of Canada. An English-speaking part!

L: Can we go to class with her?

M: Yes. She **said not to worry**. She **told me to find** her as soon as we get there.

L: Which subjects do they study in French?

M: They study history and geography in French.

L: And in English?

M: Biology and physics.

L: Nice! Is **P.E.** in English or French?

M: She explained to me that **P.E. had been** both in French and in English last year but then it changed.

L: Last year? What was different last year?

M: They had two teachers, so one week was in French and the next in English!

L: Wow . . . Confusing . . .

M: It must have been, yes.

L: Can they study other foreign languages?

M: Yes. Laura **told me she might study** Chinese, Spanish or Russian. She chose Spanish but her friend Lisa chose Russian.

L: She **should have chosen** Chinese.
So many people speak that language!

M: She said she **should have chosen** Russian!

L: Why Russian?

M: So she could be in the same class as her friend Lisa!

READY TO SPEAK?

Which languages do you speak? • Do you speak two or more languages at home? • Why? • Which languages do you study? Why did you choose them? • Would you like to study other languages?

TOOL BOX

VOCABULARY AND EXPRESSIONS

2/3 = two-thirds **1/3** = one-third **3/4** = three-fourths **2/5** = two-fifths
P.E. = Physical Education = sports activities at school

GRAMMAR

Indirect speech in an introductory verb in the simple past

- **present perfect => past perfect**
  "She has already watched that movie four times."
  => She said (that) she had already watched this movie four times.
- **Imperative => to + verb/not to + verb**
  "Come here!" => He shouted at me to come over there.
  "Don't leave your bag here!" => She asked him not to leave his bag there!
- **Simple past => past perfect**
  "I baked a wonderful cherry tart yesterday."
  => They said I had baked a wonderful cherry tart yesterday.

- **May => might**

  "My best friend may come for a pyjama party."

  => My parents said my best friend might come for a pyjama party.
- **Should => should**

  "You should plan a trip to Greece."

  => My mother said I should plan a trip to Greece.

What a day at school!

I'm usually not very keen on going to school but this one is so different. Laura **looked after** us so everything went smoothly! She and her friends took us to Lamèque Island for the weekend. There is so much to do there. We visited a small church painted inside entirely with pastel colours. We walked through **peat bog** landscapes.

We also **made for** the beach so we could fly kites. Laura and Lisa were very good at it! Marc wanted to try kayaking but he had a really hard time and eventually got wetter than ever! In the afternoon, we watched some birds. We **put off** the visit to the **arboretum**. We also had dinner on the island. We tasted sea shellfish. They were tasty and delicious.

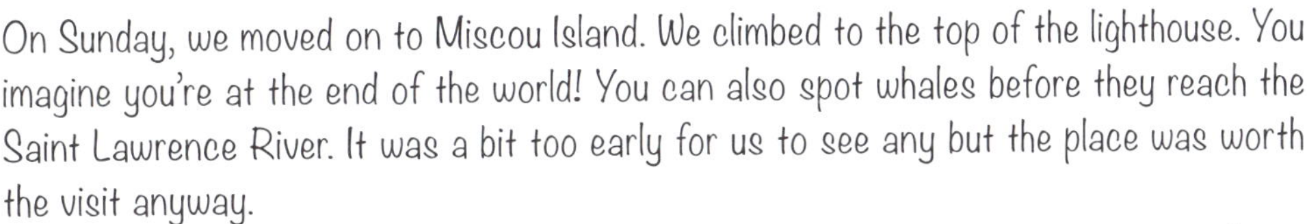

On Sunday, we moved on to Miscou Island. We climbed to the top of the lighthouse. You imagine you're at the end of the world! You can also spot whales before they reach the Saint Lawrence River. It was a bit too early for us to see any but the place was worth the visit anyway.

Lucie

TOOL BOX

VOCABULARY AND EXPRESSIONS

peat bog = a wet area with a lot of decomposed plants, especially moss

arboretum = a place for the preservation of trees

GRAMMAR

Phrasal verbs = verb + preposition

The preposition changes the meaning of the verb:

Look at = watch, view **Look for** = search **Look after** = to take care of

Put = place something somewhere

Put away = sort out/clear things away **Put off** = do something later

Put on = dress oneself => put clothes on

Make for = head for = go to **Make of** = express your opinion about something

Make over = to renovate, renew

The preposition can go either before or after the object.

She turned the TV on./She turned on the TV.

DID YOU KNOW?

- You can visit the New Brunswick Potato World Museum in Florenceville-Bristol.
- Annual snowfall in New Brunswick is between 2 and 4 metres.
- You can find the world's longest covered bridge (390 metres) in New Brunswick.

You are now ready to practise your grammar! Open your exercise book at **page 43**.

A Ride to **Cork**

Maureen: Hurry up, Dad! Speed up! We're going to be late!!!

Father: Who are these guys you want to drive to Cork?

M: Marc and Lucie? I met them on the Internet.

F: On the Internet? I told you to be careful with the Internet!

M: I'm careful, Dad . . .

F: Well . . . You never know who is behind the screen. Could be anyone!

M: Yes, Dad, I know but don't worry. Marc and Lucie are real and serious people.

F: How do you know?

M: They won an official international contest. It was in the newspaper.

F: Ohhhhh. If it was in the newspaper . . .

M: A serious newspaper, Dad! Lucie and Marc have already visited Africa, Australia, New Zealand, the US and Canada!

F: All those countries? And now, here they are, in Ireland!

M: Yes. They are touring English-speaking countries to meet young people from all around the world.

F: And you're one of them!

M: Yes! They ask people to **help them visit** different places and **meet** local people.

F: Do I have to **meet them**?

M: Yes of course! We will pick them up here in Kilkenny and drive them to Cork city centre.

F: Do they want to visit Cork?

M: Yes. I want to **have them visit the old city centre**!

F: That's a good idea. It's a nice place with a lot of good restaurants!

M: I know. They could write something about Cork on their blog.

F: Oh . . . They have a blog! What else do you want them to do?

M: I would like them to discover **Gaelic football**.

F: You cannot make them play if they don't want to!

M: I'm sure they will feel like trying. They seem quite sporty: they rode bikes and horses and tried stand-up paddle boarding.

F: And **Gaelic football** is one of our best traditions! They need to try it!

M: True.

F: OK. Are you going to **introduce them to your brother**?

M: Yes. I think I will take them to his boat. I'll **have him tell them some good stories**!

F: You'll **make them sick**!

M: No! We will just **drop in**, not go fishing with him!

F: All right!

M: Turn left, Dad. Lucie and Marc are waiting for us on the main square, in front of the castle.

F: OK. Let's wait for them.

M: No need to. Here they are . . . Lucie? Marc?

Peter: Hmm . . . No. I'm Peter and this is Mary. Are you looking for Marc and Lucie? They've gone to the toilets. They just took a boat and . . . I think Marc was sick!

READY TO SPEAK?

Have you ever shown someone around your town?
How was it? • What did you do? • If not, would you like to?
What would you do?

VOCABULARY AND EXPRESSIONS

Gaelic football = a game combining soccer and rugby, played by two teams of 15 members each

drop in = visit someone briefly and informally

GRAMMAR

Causative verbs **=> to encourage someone to do something**

To make + someone + verb + something:

I made my brother do my homework.

To let + someone + verb + something:

She let him come to her party.

To have + someone + verb + something:

They had their children wash the car.

Cork and the south coast were terrific!

We met Maureen and her father. We also met Maureen's brother, who lives on a boat. He and Maureen **get on** so well together. Not like me and my brother! He told us fantastic stories of his voyages but I'm not sure he did not **make** them **up**!

Maureen **set up** a visit of the Viking Museum on the way as we pass through Waterford. I thought the Vikings went to England and France but I did not know they went that far! In fact, they went as far as what is now Russia and even to Northern America.
At lunchtime, we **picked out** a restaurant. I took ***gudge*** as a dessert. Not bad! A bit thick maybe . . .

Then, we went for a walk in the city centre. Maureen **pointed out** the major buildings, telling us about them. We would have liked to stay longer with Maureen and her family but we needed to head for Tralee, in the southwest of Ireland. Talk to you soon!

Marc

TOOL BOX

VOCABULARY AND EXPRESSIONS

terrific = great, stunning

gudge = a traditional dessert from Ireland which looks like crumble. Also called gur cake.

county = administrative area

There are 32 counties in Ireland: 26 in the Republic and 6 in Northern Ireland.

GRAMMAR

Phrasal verbs => verb + preposition

The preposition changes the meaning of the verb.

get on with (someone) = have a good relationship
get over (something) = recover from
get away with (something) = to not get caught
get rid of (something) = remove/throw something away
get out of (doing something) = avoid something you don't want to do
make up = invent a story or lie
pick out = choose
point out = call attention to
set up = arrange

DID YOU KNOW?

- Annie Moore, from Cork **County**, was the first person to land on Ellis Island, in New York Bay. Another 2 million Irish immigrants moved to the US during the 19th century.
- Sir Walter Raleigh planted the first potato in Ireland in around 1588. Potatoes originally come from the South American continent!
- The only cable car over open water in Europe is situated in Cork **County**.

You are now ready to practise your grammar! Open your exercise book at **page 48**.

EPISODE 20

Surfing **Ireland!**

Marc: Look at this one!

Lucie: And that one!

M: There! There!
There's another one!

L: Where? I can't see . . .

M: There!

L: Oh . . . I didn't see him . . . or her.

M: Him or her?

L: I don't know. I can't see from here.

M: Well . . . You cannot know if they're male or female.

L: What? Oh . . . I thought you were talking about kite surfers.

M: No. I was talking about the dolphins. Over there.

L: Oh . . . I can't see them. They're too far away and I don't have **binoculars**.

M: Oops . . . Sorry, I thought you could. Do you want to use mine?

L: Yes. Thank you. Oh yes! There!

M: This spot is just perfect to observe animals. Look at those birds!

L: Seagulls, I think. The view is just fantastic!

M: You know, there are so many dolphins here that it's hard to **avoid** them.

L: Well . . . It is the best place to observe them, and the dolphin called Fungie is very popular.

M: Yes but it is sometimes much too touristy.

L: You know . . . Popular places often attract a lot of tourists. It's nice for the economy but not always for the landscape and wild fauna . . .

M: Yes. And that's why I wanted to come here so much!

L: Because of the tourists?

M: No! Because there're dolphins!

L: Obviously, this is a very popular place for surfing as well.

M: Yes. The **endless** waves **allow people to** surf for hours.

L: I'm not good at surfing but I admire people who can do it!

M: It requires a lot of balance and concentration.

L: That's maybe **what I lack**!

M: You don't when you take pictures! You're very concentrated then.

L: True. It must depend on the activities!

M: So I don't need **to persuade you to** take pictures of the dolphins?

L: No. Let's go to the harbour and hire a boat.

M: First, help me up! I've been sitting here for too long!

L: Watching people surfing and dolphins swimming has made you tired!

M: Well . . . Admiring such a beautiful view and looking at dolphins is tiring!

TOOL BOX

READY TO SPEAK?

What do you like doing at the seaside? • Do you like playing sports or do you prefer people-watching?
Make at least five sentences.

VOCABULARY AND EXPRESSIONS

binoculars = object with two lenses which allows you to see things far away.
avoid = to deliberately stay away from
endless = with no end = that never stops
what I lack = what I don't have, what I'm missing

GRAMMAR

Causative verbs => to encourage someone to do something

- **Force + someone + to + do + something**
  My dad forced me to clean my room.
- **Allow + someone + to + verb + something**
  My mother allows me to walk the dog in the park.
  ⚠ Allow + verb -ing if no object
  My parents don't allow smoking in the house.
- **Persuade + someone + to + verb + something**
  My cousin persuaded me to go to the library.
- **Help + someone + (to) + verb + something**
  Help me to carry this bag, please!
  Help me carry this bag, please!
  No difference in meaning.

Poetry? A piece of Ireland!

We had a great time in Dingle with Fungie the dolphin but we needed to move on to Limerick.

We were there to meet Liam. Liam is 16 years old and goes to secondary school where he studies all subjects in the Irish language. He **writes poetry**. He is **the** official poet of *The Funny* **Leprechaun**, a pub near his home. Each Saturday evening, he brings **new poems**. **The** poem I liked the most was entitled *The valley I walk in*. It deals with **the** countryside around Limerick and what it is like to live there.

We had a drink together after he performed. He told us that poetry was a part of his life. He said that he was certainly influenced by his grandfather, who was a storyteller. He used to tell Liam stories about Ireland: **legends, songs, historical stories**. All this has influenced his own writing.

Lucie and I were very impressed by his **involvement** in poetry. For us, poetry is something you study at school, something long-dead people wrote centuries ago. For Liam, it's now!

Marc

VOCABULARY AND EXPRESSIONS

leprechaun = small person, usually described as a small man with a pot of gold

involvement = participating seriously in something

TOOL BOX

GRAMMAR

Singular form

No article => general concept: I like going to ø college.

No definite article => specific thing: I like going to the college close to home.

Plural form

No definite article => general plural: ø Boys like playing football. (In fact, some don't!)

Article => specific thing: The boys in the class like playing football.

DID YOU KNOW?

- Dingle is famous for its brightly painted houses. In the 1970s, local residents decided to win the Tidy Town competition, where towns and villages are made as pretty as possible.
- There are more than 7,000 pubs in Ireland. You don't only drink beer in a pub. You also socialise, watch Gaelic football or rugby matches and play darts.
- There are ten places called Limerick . . . in the United States. A lot of Irish people emigrated to the US in the 19th century because of the agricultural and economic crisis in Ireland.

You are now ready to practise your grammar! Open your exercise book at **page 49**.

EPISODE
21

Do You Speak **Gaelic?**

Lucie: Should we go there and have lunch?

Marc: The Red Dragon? Yes. Seems nice to me.

L: Good morning.

Cadell: *Dia dhuit.**

M: It must be Gaelic . . .

L: I guess so.

C: *An féidir liom rud éigin a sheirbheáil ort?***

Neil: Cadell! Stop it! You can see they're foreigners! Come this way! I'm Neil. Have a seat.

*Good morning/** Can I get you anything?

L: Thank you! We thought **we would never find** someone who spoke English.

N: Cadell **should have been** nicer to you. There are often tourists here. He **should be used** to it!

M: Certainly not. We can't be the first foreigners to come in.

N: Surely not but it's a very small village here and most people speak Gaelic on an everyday basis.

L: When we visited Galway, we didn't have this problem.

N: Galway is a big tourist city with lots of students from all around the world!

Alana: *Dia dhuit*! Hello! I'm Alana!

M: I'm Marc and this is Lucie.

N: Alana is my sister. She's always late!

A: Yes but you know I always get there in the end!

N: Cadell spoke to them in Gaelic.

A: Naughty him! He **could have spoken** to you in English.

N: Are you here for long?

L: Just a few days . . . We'd like to visit the Connemara lakes.

A: That's certainly one of the nicest places in Ireland.

N: We should take them to the Cliffs of Moher.

A: You're right! That's a **breathtaking place**.

M: We were going to go but Lucie **suffers from** vertigo.

N: Oops. You can't even stand at the bottom of the cliffs as you'd be in the sea!

A: Lucie, I can take you to the Clare Museum in Ennis while Marc and Neil go to the cliffs, if you want.

N: Great idea! The museum's really interesting. You can learn a lot about Clare!

L: That sounds great to me! Thank you so much!

A: OK. Let's begin with the lakes. Would you like to ride a Connemara pony to go there?

L: Ponies . . . I don't know.

M: Come on, Lucie! I know you don't like horses but you did well in the Midwest.

L: I didn't fall off but I didn't like it much.

A: Well . . . They are ponies, not horses . . . And I promise we won't get too close to the lake so you won't fall in.

READY TO SPEAK?

Have you ever been to a country whose language you didn't speak? How did you manage to communicate? • If you haven't, how do you think you could make yourself understood?

VOCABULARY AND EXPRESSIONS

breathtaking = an impressive, incredibly beautiful

suffer + from have an illness => She suffers from anaemia.

TOOL BOX

TOOL BOX

GRAMMAR

Expressing something in the past with a modal

- **Structure => modal + have + past participle**

  My neighbour should have mowed the grass, his garden looks like the jungle.

  It must have rained hard here. There are muddy puddles everywhere.

  He could have come earlier to have time to visit his grandmother.

  They should have spent more time on their work.

  They would have had a better mark.

- **The -ing form is also possible:**

  Structure => modal + have + been + verb -ing

  She must have been waiting for a long time. She looks very upset!

Neil was definitely right!

I **did** have a great time at the Cliffs of Moher. The place is amazing and Neil told me about all the legends which **surround** the area. Ireland is really rich in traditional folklore! Lucie had a great time at the Clare Museum and really enjoyed riding Connemara ponies at the lakes. She **did** enjoy the exhibitions and learnt about the different traditions of County Clare. On the following day, we went to Craggaunowen (a name I still cannot pronounce properly!) This village is a reconstruction of an ancient Celtic **settlement**. It really **does** take you into the past. You can visit the castle but also live like Bronze Age settler. Clare is a really authentic area and the Connemara lakes are fascinating. The weather was rainy but the place was beautiful anyway! It was a bit cold as well . . . Well, I think that what we enjoyed the most was definitely the hot chocolate and shortbread biscuits at the local tea room!

Marc

VOCABULARY AND EXPRESSIONS

surround = relate to

settlement = a previously uninhabited area where people chose to live and build their houses.

GRAMMAR

Do + verb => to insist on the verb

You can use the simple present or simple past tenses.

Didn't you eat some of my mother's cake? Oh yes. And I did like it!

She actually does like running even though she did not want to go today.

DID YOU KNOW?

- The Claddagh ring is an international symbol of love and friendship.
- Peter O'Toole was born in Galway. The Hollywood actor holds the world record for most Oscar nominations: eight. But he never won any!
- Muckanaghederdauhaulia, in Galway County, is the longest place name in Ireland.

You are now ready to practise your grammar! Open your exercise book at **page 51**.

EPISODE 22

A Step towards **Tourism**

Lucie: I **couldn't wait to visit** this place!

Marc: I know! It's just magic!

Woman: The Giant's Causeway is one of Ireland's main tourist spots.

M: True. Are you Irish?

Woman: No. I'm Swedish. We're touring Ireland with my two sons.

M: Oh nice!

Woman: Yes. Have a wonderful day!

L: Thanks. You too.

M: I **expected to see** a lot of people but not this many.

Man: There are always this many people at this time of year.

L: Really? Do you live in the area?

Man: No. We are from the Netherlands but we've already come here several times. We love this place. Enjoy your visit!

M: Thank you . . . This is crazy. There are only tourists here.

L: Come this way. There are fewer people over there.

M: OK, let's go down there.

L: I **would like to take** some pictures with no tourists in them!

Man: Oh sorry! I'm going back up!

M: Be careful not to slip. The steps are really wet.

Man: Thanks. I have international insurance but I would **hate to go back** to Australia before the end of the European tour!

M: Sure! Have a safe trip!

L: Look at that person up there! What is that flag he's waving?

M: I don't know but he **wants everyone to know** he's here!

L: He thinks he's on the Moon.

Woman: Hi. **Sorry for** bothering you . . .
Would you mind taking a picture of my **fiancé** and me?

L: Sure. Where are you from?

Woman: Nigeria. It's our first trip to Europe.

L: There you go! Have a nice trip!

M: Look at all these people taking selfies.

L: One of them is going to fall one of these days.

M: You're right! My God.
I'm wondering if we'll find any Irish people here.

L: I'm not sure. Even the girl at the Visitor Centre was from Lithuania and the guy at the cafeteria was a student from Brazil.

M: Here look! I think I've found the only Irish representatives here!

L: Don't be so sure!
Those birds might come from Scotland or Norway, you know!

TOOL BOX

READY TO SPEAK?

Have you ever been to a very touristy place? • Did you like it? Have you ever gone to a different beach or wood to get away from people? • Do you like being around lots of people because you can make new friends?

VOCABULARY AND EXPRESSIONS

fiancé (a man) and **fiancée** (a woman) have an accent on the "e" (like café) because they come from French

sorry for + verb -ing => Sorry for asking you that but I needed to know!

GRAMMAR

Infinitive clauses

- **Can't wait to + verb/couldn't wait to + verb** => being excited/impatient

  I can't wait to try this new video game.
- **Expect + (someone) + to + verb => suppose**

  She was expecting her mother to understand her problems.
- **Would like + (someone) + to + verb => wish**

  They would like him to come on Sunday.
- **Hate + to + verb => dislike as the result of an action**

  I hate to tell you that you fail your exams.

  ⚠ Hate + verb -ing => dislike in a general way (due to experience)

  => I hate swimming.
- **Want + (someone) + to + verb => strong will**

  You want me to help you with this exercise.

Wow! What a crowd . . .

I still cannot believe it! The Giant's Causeway is **no doubt** popular because of the legend which surrounds it! In fact, the site consists of tall basalt columns and has a volcanic source. Whatever its origin, this place is **one of a kind**.

On the following day, we went to Belfast. This large city was the centre of a long sectarian conflict, which people prefer to call the Troubles. Protestant people were **told not to go** to the Catholic part of the city. And Catholics were **ordered not to take up** jobs in the civil service. The situation was really tricky and problematic . . . It began in the 1960s and ended in 1998 with a peace agreement. What is terrible is that, during this period, more than 3,500 people, both soldiers and civilians, died.

But Belfast is also the city where the Titanic was built. We visited the Titanic Museum. It was really a moving visit. We learnt everything about the making of the ship and its tragic story but we could also walk in reconstructed cabins. And, believe it or not, you can also . . . get married in the museum!

Lucie

VOCABULARY AND EXPRESSIONS

a crowd = a lot of people
no doubt = for sure
one of a kind = unique

GRAMMAR

Infinitive clauses

- **Prefer to + verb => expressing a choice over something else, wish**

  She prefers to watch foreign language films.

  ⚠ prefer + verb -ing => focusing on the experience itself

  She prefers reading to writing.

- **Ask + (someone) + to + verb**

  They asked him to come early.

- **Order + (someone) + to + verb**

  He was ordered to come quickly.

- **Negative form** => not to

  They asked him not to come early.

  He was ordered not to come quickly.

DID YOU KNOW?

- The filming of *Game Of Thrones* employed more local people in Northern Ireland than the civil service.
- Ireland lies about 20 km from the Mull of Kintyre on the Scottish coastline.
- The pneumatic tire was invented by John Boyd Dunlop (who was in fact Scottish) in Belfast in 1888.

You are now ready to practise your grammar! Open your exercise book at **page 56**.

Commonwealth? Common Fun!

Lucie: Hurry up, Marc! We're **gonna** be late!

Marc: Wait for me, Lucie. I cannot run! I'm still too **seasick**!

L: Sorry about that. It's true that you were very pale on the boat.

M: Oh please . . . Let's not talk about it!

L: The trip was not very long, though . . .

M: Too long for me, for sure.

L: Come on! It must be this way. We're almost there! It's this building! The University College Isle of Man.

Alister: Lucie?

L: Alister? Thanks for welcoming us to . . . to . . . What do you call it?

A: The Commonwealth of Youth! It is a **Yearly gathering** of teenagers from different countries of the Commonwealth.

M: What's the Commonwealth?

A: The Commonwealth is a political association of fifty-four countries.

L: Wow. Fifty-four! That's a lot!

A: Yes. They meet regularly and cooperate on trade and also organise the Commonwealth Games . . .

L: A bit like the European Union.

M: A bit like the Olympic Games.

A: A bit like all that, yes!

M: Where are these countries?

A: All around the world: Europe, America but also Oceania, Africa and Asia.

L: So . . . Everywhere, really!

A: Yes. Almost all of them are former British colonies.

M: The former Empire of Queen Victoria!

A: Yes. We're lucky to be **able to gather** together and share our cultures!

M: And what else?

A: We discuss environmental and immigration issues, for example.

L: That must be very interesting.

A: Yes. Last year, we **were able to write** proposals that we then sent to the Queen!

M: Are there representatives of all fifty-four countries?

A: No. Not everybody **was able to come**.

L: Who came this year?

A: We have members from Botswana and Uganda . . . from Malaysia and Sri Lanka . . . And also from Malta and Singapore. And many others I don't remember . . . But, um, there're about thirty-five of us this year!

L: That's a lot for such a small island!

A: True but it does not always take place on the Isle of Man. We change countries every year. Last year, I **was able to visit** Jamaica!

M: Wow! Nice trip!

A: Yes. This annual meeting is a place for debate but also for fun!

M: I would love to be part of the Commonwealth.

L: You know Marc, this **gathering** is a serious meeting to discuss important issues. It's not just a way to visit new countries!

READY TO SPEAK?

Have you ever gone on school trips? • Did you stay with a host family or on campus? • What type of activities did you do?

TOOL BOX

VOCABULARY AND EXPRESSIONS

gonna = Informal contraction of "going to", often used in American English

seasick = ill when you're on a boat

yearly = annually = which takes place once a year

gathering = meeting

GRAMMAR

Capacity to do something => **To be able to + verb**

- **Simple present**
  I am able to swim 25 metres. (= I can swim 25 metres)
- **Future**
  Tomorrow, I will be able to finish my homework. (in the future tense, you cannot use "can")
- **Simple past**
  My parents were able to send us some money.
  My brother was able to come because he was on holiday.
- **Present perfect**
  We hope you have been able to enjoy some free time this summer.

Hi everyone!

Our trip to the Isle of Man was really special! We attended some great meetings, and today's discussion was really interesting. The members mainly talked about how to protect the environment through local action. They had a lot of wonderful ideas that they already use in their own countries. They'll be able to send their proposals to the queen, as they did last year. This is a very important initiative that takes a lot of **involvement** and **commitment**.

We were also able to chat with members before and after the meetings. They're very **open-minded** teenagers. They were first chosen locally by their peers and then elected nationally. It's really satisfying to be elected but it's also a big responsibility to represent your country and all its teenagers.

The members will probably carry on helping things move forward for years to come. In fact a lot of former young representatives are now politicians working in their own communities. I think this shows the importance of the event. We may be able to go and meet them next year ... in India! That would be another great trip!

Lucie

TOOL BOX

VOCABULARY AND EXPRESSIONS

involvement = participation, to participate in an activity
commitment = when you are dedicated to a cause or an activity
open-minded = someone who loves new ideas
chat = to discuss informally **peers** = someone who is your equal
"its teenagers" refers to the country's teenagers => both pronouns ("its" and "her") can be used for a country.

GRAMMAR

Capacity to do something **=> replace "can" when you cannot use it!** (You cannot put two modals one after another.)

Will: I will be able to play next weekend's match.

Must: => You must be able to swim if you go sailing.

Should: => They should be able to improve their level of Chinese.

May: She may be able to help you with your homework.

Could: => I'm so hungry I could be able to eat hundreds of burgers!

DID YOU KNOW?

- The Isle of Man is home to several famous people, including the Bee Gees (music band) and Mark Cavendish (champion cyclist).
- The first Commonwealth Games were organised in Canada in 1930. 400 players from 11 countries participated.
- The Manx cat has no tail! These cats are so popular that they are on Isle of Man coins along with the Queen!

You are now ready to practise your grammar! Open your exercise book at **page 57**.

EPISODE 24

A Touch of **Wales**

Lucie: Can you believe that it is the last stage of our trip . . .

Marc: Yes. We **have to make** the most of it!

L: I'm glad Wales was included in our tour.

M: Me too. The landscapes are just fantastic! Look at those colours!

L: And those are lovely sheep!

M: I'm glad it's our last **leg**.

L: Why? You want to go back home? Already? I would have loved to keep on travelling for a few more weeks!

M: We **had to take** another boat to come here.

L: True! You won't **have to take** anymore now . . . That's over!

M: That's good news!

L: What is our plan for Wales?

M: OK. Let's see . . . First, Anglesey.

L: Isn't that an island??? No boats, I hope!

M: Don't worry. I'll be fine. There's a bridge!

L: OK! And then?

M: We'll visit a **copper** mine from the Bronze Age and then, we'll take the bus and go down to . . . Aberystwyth.

L: I'm not sure that's the **proper** pronunciation . . .

M: Me neither . . . There're too many consonants **in a row**.

L: We'll ask people there to pronounce it for us!

M: Right! Then we'll go to Cardiff. We'll meet Ed and Molly who will introduce us to Welsh dancing.

L: That will be fun.

M: Yes! And we'll visit the Millennium Stadium!

L: Well . . . I'll go and visit the medieval castle, I think. There's an old part and the rest was rebuilt in the 19th century. A bit like a film set!

M: Up to you! If you prefer old stones to modern technology!

L: I'm not sure I feel like leaving Snowdonia National Park. It's so quiet . . . Well . . . Except for the sheep!

M: Did you know this mountain is the highest place in Wales?

L: This is a mountain? It's more like a hill . . .

M: Shh! You'll upset the sheep!

L: Let's relax and enjoy our last **leg**!

M: You're right. We **have had to visit** so many places, write so many blog posts and meet so many people!

L: Yes. That was definitely the best part of our trip. Meeting young people our age and finding out about them, their dreams and their everyday life!

M: Yes, yes, Bob. It was very nice meeting you, too.

L: True. But Bob's conversation is a bit monotonous!

READY TO SPEAK?

Play with a friend. What do you have to do in your everyday life? Make up at least 5 sentences each and compare your answers.

TOOL BOX

VOCABULARY AND EXPRESSIONS

copper = sort of metal **proper** = correct
in a row = directly one after the other **leg** = step/stage

GRAMMAR

Obligation to do something => replace "must" when you cannot use it! => To have to + verb

- **Simple present** => I have to clean my room. = I must clean my room.
I mustn't clean my room. = It is forbidden for me to clean my room.
I don't have to clean my room = it is not necessary to clean my room.
- **Simple past** => I had to give her a present.
- **Present perfect** => I have had to look after my younger brother for hours.

Take a deep breath!

Llanfairpwllgwyngyllgogerychwyrndrobwllllantysiliogogogoch! Do you know what that is? It's the longest place name in an English-speaking country. The village itself is **tiny**, with nothing special but it is famous worldwide for its name! I **will have to learn** how to pronounce it properly! That's one of the funniest things in Wales! We **would have to wait** for another trip to learn more Welsh. When in Cardiff, everyone **should have to try** Welsh dancing. They **may have to take** several lessons because, in fact, it is quite difficult. That's the case for any kind of traditional dance, I guess. Marc visited the stadium and I visited the castle... And we were both happy with our visits! When we left Wales, we crossed a bridge. I wanted to take a boat to Bristol but...

You know Marc by now! What is funny is that you have to pay a **toll** to cross the bridge when you come from England to Wales but not when you go from Wales to England. That's certainly a **reminder** of the rivalry between England and Wales!

Lucie

VOCABULARY AND EXPRESSIONS

tiny = very very small

toll = money you have to pay to use some roads and bridges

reminder = a thing that causes someone to remember something

GRAMMAR

Obligation to do something => replace "must" when you cannot use it! (You cannot put two modals one after another.)

- **Will**: I **will have to listen** to this song again. I didn't hear the words!
- **Should**: All students **should have to respect** the same rules during exams.
- **May:** He **may have to try** several times before passing his driving test.
- **Would:** You **would have to wait** for ages for a bus to come.

DID YOU KNOW?

- There are four times as many sheep as humans in Wales!
- There is a Welsh-speaking community in Argentina, owing to the arrival of immigrants from Wales in the 19th century.
- Daffodils and leeks are symbols of Wales.

You are now ready to practise your grammar! Open your exercise book at **page 59**.

EPISODE 25

Time to **Go Home**

Marc: Can you believe it, Lucie?

Lucie: No, I can't!

M: This is the end!
We've visited so many places!

L: Yes, I know! I loved meeting all those people . . .

M: Nelson, Archie, Neil . . .

L: Kasia, Aishling and Anahera . . .

M: And let's not forget Bob the Sheep!

L: I think he is the one I'll miss the most!

M: You know, our blog received a lot of nice comments!

L: Yes. I've read some of them and people really enjoyed reading about our adventures!

M: I enjoyed writing about them.

L: Me too!

M: I think they also really liked your pictures and drawings. That was a real plus for the blog!

L: Thank you. I loved doing that too! I usually paint for myself so it was nice for once to share my art with people I don't know.

M: What will you do when you get back home?

L: I don't know . . . First, I'll kiss my little sister and then spend time with my family and friends.

M: You're right. We've been away from home for several months now.

L: And you? What will you do?

M: Same as you. And I'll also organise all the pictures I took.

L: God! That's going to take you years. Do you know how many you took?

M: I'm not sure. Probably more than 10,000. I uploaded them as I went but I now need to organise them all . . . Maybe I'll add some more pictures to our blog.

L: I think we will remember this trip forever.

M: For sure! We'll need to visit some new countries soon!

L: We're not even back home yet and you already want to go away again?

M: Of course! I got used to you, you know. It's going to be weird not to see you every day!

L: True. I'll miss you too. But I don't think I'll miss your sense of humour!

M: Be nice to me, please!

L: OK! Let's check our luggage in. It's almost time to board.

M: My suitcase . . . My suitcase? My suitcase!

L: What about your suitcase? I told you I don't like your sense of humour sometimes.

M: I'm not kidding! Oh no!!! I left it in the taxi!

L: Oh Marc . . . We'll miss our flight. You could have found another way if you wanted to stay here longer!

READY TO SPEAK?

Which episode was your favourite? • Why?
Are there other countries you'd like to visit? • Which of the places Marc and Lucie visited would you like to visit the most? • Why?

This is the end! Our trip is over!

You cannot imagine how sad we are to leave you. Thank you so much to all of you for all your nice comments and your sweet emoticons. We really enjoyed sharing our feelings, pictures and paintings with you. We know you liked them a lot and that some of you sent us your own drawings. It was charming to see how interested you were in our trip!

We hope we made you feel like travelling and visiting new and unusual places. You know you don't necessarily need to go far away. We're sure there are interesting things to discover and people to meet close to your home. Adventure is sometimes at the end of your street!

It's also time to thank the organisers of this trip! They trusted us and made a wonderful programme for us. We could not have dreamed of a better experience. Don't hesitate to read our blog again and follow our trip on a map! We will travel again together for sure, so stay in touch because we'll keep you posted about our next trip! Lots of love to all!

Marc and Lucie

PS: Oh, by the way . . . The taxi driver brought Marc's suitcase in time!

DID YOU KNOW?

- In Mexico, Tijuana International Airport is on the border between Mexico and the USA. It is the only airport in the world which has a terminal in two countries, one in Mexico and one in the US.
- A store in the US city of Alabama specialises in selling items found in unclaimed airport luggage.
- At Johannesburg airport, the staff discovered a very smelly box . . . It contained 1,600 snakes and frogs.

You are now ready to practise your grammar! Open your exercise book at **page 64**.

Exercises
and *Check your Skills*

Nolwena Monnier • Ève Grosset

Editorial concept and graphical design: Okidokid - www.okidokid.fr

EPISODE 01

A New Hope!

EXERCISE 1

Listen to or read the dialogue again and complete the following table:

	TRUE	FALSE
Lucie and Marc won a world tour of English-speaking countries.		
Lucie and Marc know about their programme.		
Marc wants to taste hamburgers.		
Lucie does not want to go.		
Marc is happy about writing a blog.		

EXERCISE 2

Read the blog entry and answer the following questions:

1 • Where is Marc from?

---

2 • How old is Lucie?

---

3 • What types of countries will Marc and Lucie visit?

---

4 • What will Marc and Lucie post on their blog?

---

5 • Is Lucie a good painter?

EXERCISE 3

Link the two parts of the sentences:

Marc and Lucie	O	O	do you like visiting?
Do you like	O	O	texts and pictures.
What types of monuments	O	O	discovering new places?
Marc and Lucie met	O	O	are friends.
The blog will contain	O	O	last year in Egypt.

EPISODE 02

Road Trip

EXERCISE 1

Listen to or read the dialogue again and choose the correct answer:

1 • Lucie and Marc will leave in:
a. February.
b. May.
c. July.

2 • Lucie and Marc will first visit:
a. Nigeria.
b. Australia.
c. England.

3 • What is a Tasmanian devil?
a. A deep lake.
b. A type of food.
c. An animal.

4 • What's special about Matamata?
a. It's in a movie.
b. A lord lives there.
c. You can watch movies there.

5 • How does Lucie know about Nunavut?
a. She has already been there.
b. It's a place famous for Native Indian art.
c. There is a large white bear community.

6 • What will they do in Tralee?
a. Stay.
b. Move.
c. Surf.

7 • Where is the Isle of Man?
a. In Wales.
b. In Northern Ireland.
c. Off the coasts of Ireland and the UK.

EXERCISE 2

Read the blog entry again and complete the following table:

	TRUE	FALSE
The trip will be very short.		
Marc is very excited to go to Australia.		
Marc wants to learn an African language.		
Lucie does not like Nunavut art.		
Lucie and Marc think all the places on the trip will be interesting to visit.		

EXERCISE 3

Complete the text with the following words:
America • happy • places • discovering • favourite • trip

Marc and Lucie are so ______. They received the programme for their ______. They will visit many ______ in Africa, Australia, New Zealand, North ______ and the British Isles. Their ______ places will certainly be Cairns (for Marc) and Nunavut (for Lucie). They like nature and art but also ______ new things, like languages.

EPISODE 03

What Does it Take to Tour the World?

EXERCISE 1

Listen to or read the dialogue again and answer the following questions in full sentences:

1 • What does Marc do? ______________________

____

2 • According to Lucie, is Marc organised? ______________________

____

3 • What did Mark put on his bed? ______________________

____

4 • Where is Mark's mobile phone? ______________________

____

5 • Where is Mark's passport? ______________________

____

6 • Is Lucie's bag ready? ______________________

____

EXERCISE 2

Link the two parts of the sentences:

Marc's suitcase O	O a German key ring.
Lucie hopes O	O is Nigeria.
Lucie went to Milan O	O is really heavy.
Marc decided to take O	O a few years ago.
Their first destination O	O she won't feel home-sick

EXERCISE 3

Read the blog entry and choose the correct answer:

1 • Lucie did not forget
a. her cuddly toy.
b. her charming brother.
c. her camera.

2 • Lucie wants to post pictures on their blog
a. every month.
b. regularly.
c. every year.

3 • Lucie's lucky charm is
a. a rubber.
b. a book.
c. a key.

4 • Marc's lucky charm is
a. a key ring.
b. a flag.
c. a German flower pot.

You are now ready to recap! Turn the page and **Check Your Skills!**

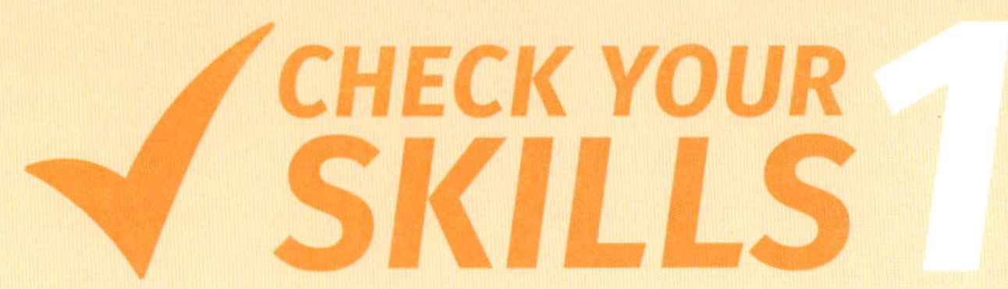

A Complete the sentences with the following words: can/mustn't/goes/will/went.

1 • Tom ______________ go to the swimming pool next Saturday.
2 • Clara ______________ to school by bike yesterday.
3 • Peter ______________ to the public garden with his dog every Sunday.
4 • I ______________ run very fast.
5 • You ______________ cross the street without looking.

B Complete the sentences with the following words: What/Where/When/How/Why.

1 • ______________ is your birthday?
2 • ______________ will you do next Monday?
3 • ______________ are you crying?
4 • ______________ are you?
5 • ______________ did you buy this book?

C Make up four sentences with exclamatory words using the adjective beautiful and the noun castle.

1 • ____
2 • ____
3 • ____
4 • ____

D Complete with the correct personal pronouns:

1 • ______________ brother said I am not organised.
2 • __________ wants to go to the swimming pool.

3 • This dog is wandering in the street. Maybe __________ is lost.
4 • My mother likes __________ job a lot.
5 • My sister and her boyfriend are on holiday. __________ are in Malawi.

E Complete the sentences with the following words: so much/so many/how much/many/too many.

1 • __________ is this t-shirt?
2 • There were __________ people at that concert that we could not dance!
3 • __________ students work to earn money.
4 • Don't put __________ water in your bath!
5 • There are __________ cars on the road! We will be late!

F Complete the sentences in a logical way:

1 • __________ boy of the class is Leo. (superlative - clever)
2 • __________ cat on Earth is my cat! (superlative - nice)
3 • Wow! This movie is __________ the one I watched last week. (comparative - interesting)
4 • This mouse is __________ a cat. (comparative - small)
5 • This place is __________ the other one. (inferiority – large)
6 • Today, I am __________ I was yesterday. (inferiority - cheerful)

G Complete with the following words: anywhere/anything/somebody/nowhere/nobody/something.

1 • __________ is knocking at the door.
2 • Did you leave __________ at school?
3 • __________ knows where he is.
4 • I cannot find my keys __________.
5 • I need __________ to fix this.
6 • We have __________ to go. All the hotels are full.

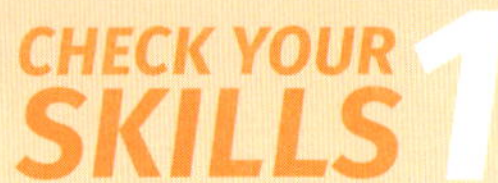

H Make up sentences with the following words, as in the example:

colour + flower + beautiful => The colour of this flower is beautiful.

1 • My father + wallet + on the table => ____________________

2 • The page + book + torn => ____________________

3 • Your grand-mother + tree + tall => ____________________

4 • The album + year + great => ____________________

Check your points!

(0.5 point for each correct sentence)

Exercise A:	______ points	Exercise E:	______ points
Exercise B:	______ points	Exercise F:	______ points
Exercise C:	______ points	Exercise G:	______ points
Exercise D:	______ points	Exercise H:	______ points
		Total:	______ **points**

Between 15 and 20 points:

Well done! You can jump to the next episode! ☺

Between 10 and 15:

Pretty good! You may need to look back over some of the Tool Boxes.

Between 5 and 10:

Oops! I think you went too fast.

You should review some basic knowledge before going on.

Between 0 and 5:

Oops! You had better review episodes 1 to 3! Keep going!

Connected Cocoa

EXERCISE 1 Listen to or read the dialogue again and choose the right answer:

1 • Dunjuma grows:
a. cocoa trees.
b. apple trees.
c. cherry trees.

2 • Dunjuma has worked with his father for:
a. 10 years.
b. 20 years.
c. 4 years.

3 • Dunjuma sells his cocoa:
a. at the local market.
b. in Europe.
c. nowhere.

4 • Dunjuma uses:
a. an electric car.
b. a motorbike.
c. a white car.

EXERCISE 2 Read the blog entry again and complete the following table:

	TRUE	FALSE
There are several official languages in Nigeria.		
There is a rainy and a dry season in Nigeria.		
You can find cocoa, banana and mango trees in Nigeria.		
Cocoa beans must be dried before people put them into big bags.		
Dunjuma's cocoa beans are exported by plane.		

EXERCISE 3 Link the two parts of the sentences:

Marc and Lucie	O	O	has an eco-friendly attitude.
Dunjuma	O	O	travel to Europe by boat.
Cocoa beans	O	O	English, Haoussa, Yoruba and Igbo.
Lagos is	O	O	ate marvellous mango fruit.
In Nigeria, people speak	O	O	the biggest city in Nigeria.

EPISODE 05

South Africa Past and Future

EXERCISE 1

Fill in the blanks with words from the dialogue:

Lucie and Marc visited Bo-Kaap in ______________ ______________. Nelson showed them ______________ houses. Nelson has a lot of ______________ there. There is a museum of slavery because many ______________ lived there some ______________ ago. Now, the area is ______________ as a National Heritage Site.

EXERCISE 2

Change the following sentences using could:

1 • I was able to understand the whole song.

____

2 • Marc can hear the sound of a river.

____

3 • We had the opportunity to see beautiful stars in the sky.

____

4 • Lucie had the chance to taste so many vegetables in her soup.

____

5 • They were capable of feeling the tension between their parents.

____

EXERCISE 3

Read the blog entry again and complete the following table:

	TRUE	FALSE
Lucie put pictures of Bo-Kaap on the blog.		
Lucie and Marc were very moved by the history of Bo-Kaap.		
Bo-Kaap is a modern place.		
Marc and Lucie went to the jungle.		
Part of the population is poor and lives in poor housing conditions.		

A Full-Time Job

EXERCISE 1

Link the two parts of the sentences:

Kilimanjaro is	O	O	became a real swamp.
Kofi is	O	O	because he loves animals.
In the 1990's, the National Park	O	O	a reserve since the 1970's.
The National Park has been	O	O	more than 5,500 metres high.
Kofi works at the park	O	O	a ranger who protects wild animals.

EXERCISE 2

Fill in the blanks with the following words:
teenagers/sky/visited/friendship/concerned.

Marc and Lucie ____________ a Maasai village. They met ____________ and listened to stories under a starlit ____________. They understood that most teenagers are ____________ with the same things: love, ____________ and their future (and the future of the planet!).

EXERCISE 3

Choose the right answer:

1 • Lucie and Marc watched:
a. dancers.
b. wild animals.
c. other tourists.

2 • Kofi took them to:
a. a traditional African village.
b. have dinner with his grandparents.
c. hunt wild animals.

3 • Marc and Lucie could:
a. listen to traditional stories.
b. taste traditional drinks.
c. see hippos.

4 • African teenagers were:
a. away in the city.
b. surprised to see Lucie and Marc.
c. not very talkative.

5 • They spoke with African teenagers and realised:
a. they were bizarre.
b. they read the same books.
c. they have a lot in common.

You are now ready to recap! Turn the page and **Check Your Skills!**

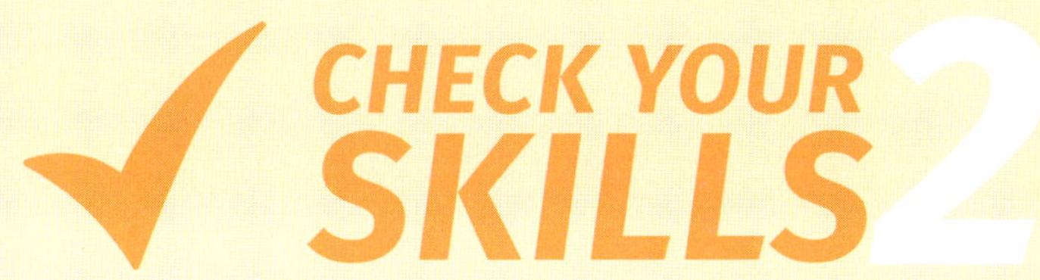

A Complete the sentences with the preterite:

1 • My parents ____________ to Venice for their wedding anniversary four years ago. (go)
2 • Mr Wilson ____________ to play golf more often than last year. (try)
3 • When I ____________ young, my favourite teacher ____________ Mrs Albert. (be)
4 • I ____________ a very nice birthday party two weeks ago. (have)

B Complete the sentences with the present perfect:

1 • I ________________ for this letter for three days. (wait)
2 • He ______________ on the phone with his friends for one hour! (speak)
3 • The children ________________ football for hours. (play)
4 • I ________________ time at the swimming pool this morning. (spend)

C Choose between preterite and present perfect:

1 • Last week, I went/have gone to my best friend's birthday party.
2 • She lived/has lived in New York for 4 years. She now lives in Dubai.
3 • Since I was born, I loved/have loved listening to music.
4 • I studied/have studied Japanese 6 years ago.

D Choose between for and since:

1 • I have played tennis for/since 3 years.
2 • This restaurant has been here for/since a long time.
3 • A lot of rain has fallen for/since the beginning of the week.
4 • This restaurant has been here for/since 2002.

E Choose between a few or a little:

1 • I only have ____________ money in my purse.

2 • ____________ children are playing in the playground.

3 • Could you give me ____________ milk?

4 • She has ____________ problems to solve.

Check your points!

(1 point for each correct sentence)

Exercise A: ________ points

Exercise B: ________ points

Exercise C: ________ points

Exercise D: ________ points

Exercise E: ________ points

Total: ________ points

Between 15 and 20 points:

Well done! You can jump to the next episode! ☺

Between 10 and 15:

Pretty good! You may need to look back over some of the Tool Boxes.

Between 5 and 10:

Oops! I think you went too fast.

You should review some basic knowledge before going on.

Between 0 and 5:

Oops! You had better review episodes 4 to 6! Keep going!

Native Art

EXERCISE 1

Link the two parts of the sentences:

Natural pigments take long to prepare,	O	O	some people prefer to make sculptures.
Instead of painting	O	O	Lucie and Marc have to go to the Parklands.
Unless you meet the artists,	O	O	you can go to the Adelaide Festival of Arts.
In order to see beautiful sculptures,	O	O	which is why some artists use industrial ones.
If you like art,	O	O	you cannot know if they use natural pigments.

EXERCISE 2

Fill in the blanks with the following words:
Australians/beach/evening/discussed/traditional.

Lucie and Marc had a wonderful ______________. In town they met a group of young ______________ and they went to the ______________ with them. They ______________ the Aboriginal situation and sang ______________ songs while watching the sunset.

EXERCISE 3

Read the blog entry again and complete the following table:

	TRUE	FALSE
Marc and Lucie only visited exhibits.		
They met a group of young Australians in the Parklands.		
All the young people were native Australians.		
European settlers were nice to Aborigines.		
Lucie and Marc enjoyed their evening on the sand a lot.		

EPISODE 08

OK Coral!

EXERCISE 1

Link the two parts of the sentences:

Lucie and Marc are meeting Archie,	O	O	to alert children to marine pollution.
The Foundation visits schools	O	O	cleaned all the plastic garbage from the beach.
The Foundation wants people	O	O	to admire the Great Barrier Reef.
The children from a nearby school	O	O	a volunteer who protects the Great Barrier Reef.
Lucie and Marc are going scuba diving	O	O	to protect the Great Barrier Reef.

EXERCISE 2

Complete the text with the following words:
dry/loved/farms/young/colourful.

Marc and Lucie ______________ scuba diving with Archie. The Great Barrier Reef is so ______________. Then, they went to the Outback, a very ______________ and unpopulated area in Central Australia. They met some ______________ students who work on ______________ during their gap year.

EXERCISE 3

Complete the following sentences using could/should or would + have + past participle:

1 • I ______________________________ to the cinema yesterday but I had exams. (to go)

2 • You ______________________________ this movie. It was really great. (to watch)

3 • My brother ______________________________ playing another sport. He really didn't like this one. (have more fun)

4 • We ______________________________ to this problem. It is too late to fix it now. (pay more attention)

Weird Animals!

EXERCISE 1

Listen to or read the dialogue again and complete the following table:

	TRUE	FALSE
Tasmania is smaller than Australia.		
Paula works for the University of Australia.		
Lucie needs her camera.		
Wombats eat meat.		
Wombats are the only protected animals in Tasmania.		

EXERCISE 2

Choose the right answer:

1 • Paula went to Sydney:
a. to sail from Sydney to Tasmania.
b. to buy a boat.
c. to watch a race.

2 • Paula's husband is crazy about car races, which is why:
a. he drives his own car.
b. he sold his bike.
c. he goes to a car race every year.

3 • In Australia, summer holidays take place in December/January because
a. people like going on holiday when it's rainy.
b. people don't live in the Northern Hemisphere.
c. people like having long holiday to celebrate Christmas.

4 • Australian schoolchildren wear:

a. whatever they want.

b. uniforms.

c. dresses.

5 • Marc would love to go to school in Australia because:

a. he could play a lot of sport.

b. he would be on holiday all the time.

c. he could give up maths.

EXERCISE 3

Change these sentences following the example:

I go to museums when I visit a large city.
=> Last year, I went to all the museums in Washington.

I play tennis every Saturday.
=> I have played tennis for two hours.

1 • I play rugby every Wednesday.

For three years, ...

2 • I go to the swimming pool on Sundays.

.... last Sunday.

3 • I watch horror movies every week.

Yesterday, ...

4 • I eat ice cream.

Since I was young, ...

5 • I paint my house.

.... for hours.

You are now ready to recap! Turn the page and **Check Your Skills!**

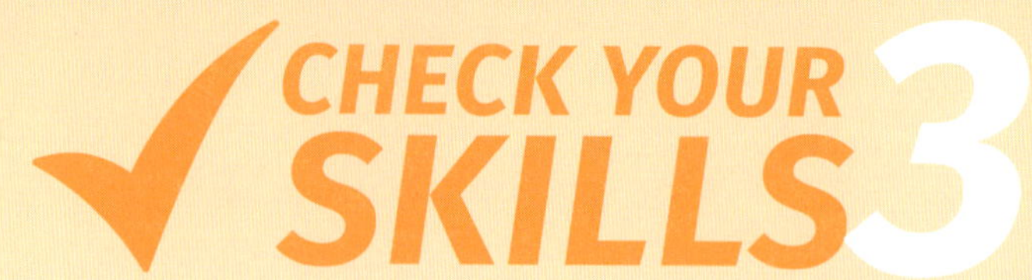

A **Complete the sentences with the following words:** **because of/however/in order to/on the contrary/therefore.**

1 • I went to the park this afternoon to meet my friends. ______________ I could not find them.

2 • "You don't like gardening?" " ______________, I love it".

3 • He did not work hard enough. ______________, he failed his English exam.

4 • ______________ get there on time, we'll take the bus.

5 • ______________ the noise, I could not hear what she said.

B **Complete the sentences with the following words:** **while/but/in front of/behind/even if.**

1 • ______________ sleeping, I dreamt about my next holiday.

2 • Your school bag? You can't see it from here. It is just ______________ the door!

3 • I need to go to the doctor ______________ I don't have time today . . .

4 • Can't you see it? It's just ______________ you, on the table.

5 • ______________ you ask me, I won't tell you.

C Make up sentences that match the drawing, based in this example:

=> Dad wants his son to clean the table.

1 • ....

2 • ....

3 • ....

4 • ....

5 • ....

D Complete with the correct tense: simple present/simple past/present perfect.

1 • Yesterday I ____________ to the cinema with my best friend. (to go)

2 • My uncle ____________ tennis since he was 6 years old. (to play)

3 • Children usually ____________ eating chocolate biscuits. (to like)

4 • My parents and I ____________ Ireland 6 years ago. (to visit)

5 • France ____________ part of the European Union for years. (to be)

Check your points!

(1 point for each correct sentence)

Exercise A: ______ points

Exercise B: ______ points

Exercise C: ______ points

Exercise D: ______ points

Total: ______ **points**

Between 15 and 20 points:

Well done! You can jump to the next episode! ☺

Between 10 and 15:

Pretty good! You may need to look back over some of the Tool Boxes.

Between 5 and 10:

Oops! I think you went too fast.

You should review some basic knowledge before going on.

Between 0 and 5:

Oops! You had better review episodes 7 to 9! Keep going!

Let's score!

EXERCISE 1

Complete the text with the following words:
popular/cricket/met/common/country.

Lucie and Marc ______________ Kasia and Ted. Kasia is a rugby player and Ted is a ______________ player. These sports are very ______________ in their ______________. It's not very ______________ for girls to play rugby but more and more are doing so. Marc does not play sports but plays video games.

EXERCISE 2

Listen to or read the dialogue again and choose the right answer:

1 • Lucie and Marc watched the match
a. with Kasia.
b. with Ted.
c. on their own.

2 • On the following day, Kasia and Marc
a. took a boat.
b. went to the beach.
c. had dinner.

3 • The teenagers had fun
a. swimming.
b. paddling.
c. fishing.

4 • They also tasted
a. a traditional pastry.
b. coffee and hot chocolate.
c. New Zealand.

EXERCISE 3

Change these sentences following the example:

My sister + read + book => My sister feels like reading this book.

1 • My brother + go + beach => ....

2 • My best friend + learn + Italian => ....

3 • I + travel + Mexico => ....

4 • They + watch + movie => ....

EPISODE 11

Welcome to New Zealand!

EXERCISE 1

Listen to or read the dialogue again and complete the following table:

	TRUE	FALSE
Anahera and Tamati both speak Maori.		
The Maori language is spoken only in New Zealand.		
The Maori language is spoken only in a family context.		
In the past, Maori used to be an oral language.		
Hangi is a traditional dance.		

EXERCISE 2

Answer the following questions:

1 • Why did Marc and Lucie go to Massey University? ________________

____

2 • Who can take courses on Maori culture? ________________

____

3 • What is included in Prof. Longworth's projects? ________________

____

4 • What did Marc try to do with the automatic translator? ________________

____

EXERCISE 3

Change these sentences to the passive form:

1 • Students can learn the Maori language language at university.

____

2 • Older people tell children about Maori legends.

____

3 • Young people don't often sing traditional songs.

____

4 • Lucie and Marc have to write the blog post before ten o'clock.

____

EPISODE
12

Lord of the Cinema!

EXERCISE 1

Listen to or read the dialogue again and choose the right answer:

1 • The name "Matamata" comes from:
a. an animal.
b. a person.
c. a tree.

2 • Why is Marc so happy?
a. It's a sunny day.
b. He wanted to taste a cupcake.
c. He is glad to visit Matamata and the Hobbit village.

3 • The cinema industry in New Zealand:
a. is just beginning.
b. has never been very important.
c. is a real advantage for the country.

4 • You need a lot of people to shoot a movie:
a. barmen, barmaids and cooks.
b. actors, technicians and makeup artists.
c. teachers, artists and gardeners.

5 • Why does Lucie think cinema is important for the area?
a. It adds magic.
b. It brings tourists.
c. It brings money.

EXERCISE 2

Link the two parts of the sentences:

Lucie and Marc loved	O	O	to come and visit the Matamata area.
Matamata has a lot more to offer	O	O	colourful and packed with animals.
Not far away, there is a small town	O	O	than just the visit to the Hobbit village.
In the autumn, the countryside is	O	O	with restaurants and places to visit.
Marc and Lucie encourage you	O	O	the Matamata area.

EXERCISE 3

Complete the text with the following words:
autumn/visit/movie/cupcake/celebrate/big.

Marc absolutely wanted to ______________ Matamata because he is a ______________ fan of *Lord of the Rings*. The ______________ was shot there. He was so happy to ______________ his birthday there. Lucie brought a ______________! They both liked the area a lot. It is natural and beautiful in the ______________.

You are now ready to recap! Turn the page and **Check Your Skills!**

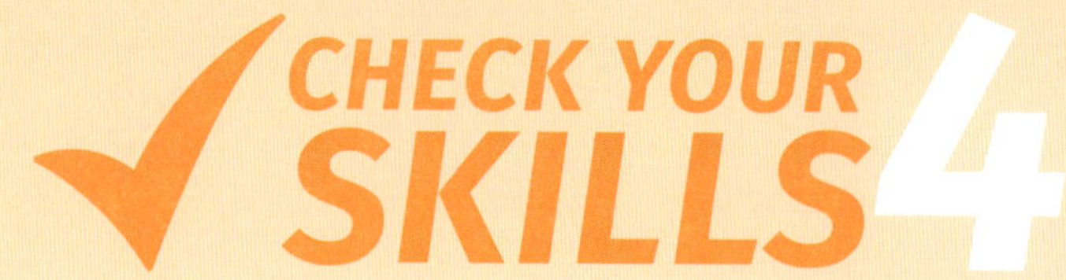

A Complete the sentences with in, on, to or from:

1 • My neighbours are going on holiday ____________ July.
2 • My brother will move ____________ Boston next September.
3 • ____________ Sundays, there is no school!
4 • Salvatore? He was born in Rio. He is ____________ Venezuela at the moment.
5 • Elizabeth I reigned ____________ the 16th century.

B Change these active sentences into passive sentences:

1 • A lot of people play basketball.

____

2 • Christopher Colombus discovered America.

____

3 • I have cleaned the whole house.

____

4 • Mr Simpson built this house in 1956.

____

5 • Clara has hit Peter.

____

C Change these active sentences into passive sentences:

1 • Only two people could understand the problem.

____

2 • My dad must repair my bike.

____

3 • The whole class would use the computer.

____

4 • We should make the cake before tomorrow.

____

5 • Peter can exchange this book.

____

D Complete the sentences choosing the right tense:

1 • I think you ______________________ tomorrow. (sleep)

2 • She guessed you ______________________ to listen to music. (like)

3 • My uncle ______________________ his nephew would be happy to play tennis. (suppose)

4 • Marc ______________________ he would be interested in visiting Matamata. (say)

5 • They ______________________ the woman will work for a few more hours. (say)

Check your points!

(1 point for each correct sentence)

Exercise A: ________ points

Exercise B: ________ points

Exercise C: ________ points

Exercise D: ________ points

Total: ________ **points**

Between 15 and 20 points:

Well done! You can jump to the next episode! ☺

Between 10 and 15:

Pretty good! You may need to look back over some of the Tool Boxes.

Between 5 and 10:

Oops! I think you went too fast.

You should review some basic knowledge before going on.

Between 0 and 5:

Oops! You had better review episodes 10 to 12! Keep going!

EPISODE 13

Flea Market Day

EXERCISE 1

Listen to or read the dialogue again and complete the following table:

	TRUE	FALSE
Portland is situated on the East Coast.		
Marc went to a flea market with his parents when he was 12.		
Lucie likes the lamp.		
Portland is one of the greenest cities in the US.		
Lucie wants to buy a necklace.		

EXERCISE 2

Answer the following questions:

1 • In Portland, what type of public transport can you use to go to work?

2 • Why do they organise flea markets?

3 • How many prizes has Portland won?

4 • Why didn't Marc want to go to a vegan restaurant?

5 • In the end, what did Marc think about vegan food?

EXERCISE 3

Make up sentences with indirect questions corresponding to the drawings:

1 . She wonders ....

2 . They don't know ....

3 . He wants to know ....

4 . She asks the man ....

5 . She wonders ....

EPISODE 14

The Middle of Nowhere

EXERCISE 1

Listen to or read the dialogue again and choose the right answer:

1 • Lucie would like to:
a. go swimming in Lake Michigan.
b. look at the horses.
c. visit museums.

2 • Aisling lives:
a. in an apartment.
b. on a farm.
c. in a town house.

3 • Marc wants to go to:
a. the national park.
b. the Indian reserve.
c. watch a movie.

4 • Aisling's farm is:
a. near a big town.
b. far from a big town.
c. in a big town.

5 • Aisling comes back from school:
a. on weekends.
b. during the holidays.
c. every evening.

EXERCISE 2

Complete the text with the following words:
sculptures/region/spaces/Park/impressed/cities.

Lucie and Marc were very ________ by the Midwest ________. They visited large open ________, an Indian reserve and Roosevelt National ________. They also went to South Dakota and had a look at the Mount Rushmore ________. They enjoyed their stay with Aishling and also getting away from the big ________.

EXERCISE 3

Link the two parts of the sentences:

I'd rather go to the swimming pool	O	O	whether Marc wants to or not.
Whether you're interested or not	O	O	or the bus to go to the cinema.
I would like to take either my bike	O	O	I will tell you about my day!
Lucie plans to visit Berlin	O	O	they'd better take their scarves.
It is so cold today that	O	O	than to school.

EPISODE 15

A Taste of New Orleans!

EXERCISE 1

Listen to or read the dialogue again and complete the following table:

	TRUE	FALSE
Tom has been living in New Orleans for a very long time.		
Tom likes the city a lot.		
Marc is really keen on visiting the Voodoo Museum.		
Lucie wants to visit a plantation.		
Marc thinks gumbo is a dance.		
Lucie knows what gumbo is.		

EXERCISE 2

Read the blog entry again and answer the following questions:

1 • What did Lucie and Marc visit in New Orleans?

---

2 • Who are the Cajuns?

---

3 • How can you tour the Mississippi?

---

4 • What did Lucie and Marc visit on the plantation?

---

5 • How did they feel on the plantation?

EXERCISE 3

Complete the sentences with the correct tense (preterite, present perfect simple, present perfect continuous or past perfect):

1 • Yesterday, my friend and I ______________ to the flea market. (go)

2 • I thought he ______________ his homework before he played football. (finish)

3 • We ______________ this trip for many years. We are so disappointed it's cancelled. (plan)

4 • My uncle ______________ football all his life. He's the best. (play)

5 • She remembered she ______________ this place when she was young. (visit)

You are now ready to recap! Turn the page and **Check Your Skills!**

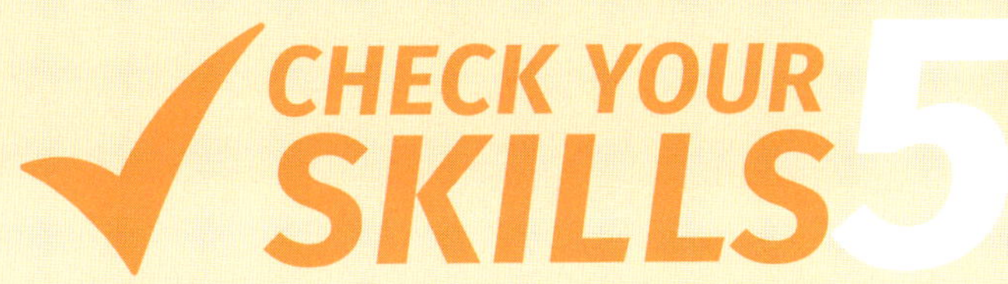

A Complete the following sentences with an indirect question:

1 • Who is singing in the street?

She is wondering ....

2 • When did you buy this new wallet?

I'm asking you ....

3 • Where is their cousin's new house?

They are wondering ....

4 • Why are you late?

You are asking ....

5 • How are you, James?

He wants to know ....

B Change the sentences using 'd rather or 'd better:

1 • You should listen to your parents!

....

2 • I would prefer to go to the mountains on holiday.

....

3 • If they had the choice, they would choose the blue one.

....

4 • I would advise her to read this new novel.

....

5 • We would recommend her not to tell them about it.

....

C Complete the following sentences with whether/or or either/or:

1 • ______ you revised ______ not, I'm sure you will succeed.

2 • ______ he wants to ______ not, he will try to solve this problem.

3 • I can take ______ meat ______ fish, I don't mind.

4 • ______ you choose this house ______ the other one, we will move to a fantastic neighbourhood.

5 • They can pick you up at the airport ______ by car ______ by taxi.

D Complete the sentences with the correct tense (preterite, present perfect simple, present perfect continuous or past perfect):

1 • My cousin and I ______ in a music festival. (participate)

2 • She ______ Japanese for several weeks, and she loves it. (study)

3 • They thought we ______ to our grandparents before they came back from the seaside. (write)

4 • He ______ on this essay for hours yesterday. (work)

5 • I remembered you ______ this movie before we met. (watch)

Check your points!

(1 point for each correct sentence)

Exercise A: ________ points

Exercise B: ________ points

Exercise C: ________ points

Exercise D: ________ points

Total: ________ points

Between 15 and 20 points:

Well done! You can jump to the next episode! ☺

Between 10 and 15:

Pretty good! You may need to look back over some of the Tool Boxes.

Between 5 and 10:

Oops! I think you went too fast.

You should review some basic knowledge before going on.

Between 0 and 5:

Oops! You had better review episodes 13 to 15! Keep going!

EPISODE
16

Please Meet . . .

EXERCISE 1

Listen to or read the dialogue again and choose the right answer:

1 • What are Marc and Lucie doing?
a. They are visiting Winnipeg.
b. They are meeting new friends.
c. They are walking to watch the aurora borealis.

2 • What does Lucie especially appreciate?
a. She appreciates silence.
b. She appreciates city life.
c. She appreciates talking.

3• What are they going to do?
a. They are going to camp.
b. They are going to play soccer.
c. They are going to fish.

4 • What does Marc want to do?
a. He wants to take pictures.
b. He wants to meet Big Foot.
c. He wants to fish in the river.

5 • What is Big Foot?
a. It is a wild animal.
b. It is a savage legendary creature.
c. It is a plant.

EXERCISE 2

Complete the text with the following words:
visit/hiking/Ana/world/enjoyed.

__________ took Lucie and Marc to the Far North, in Canada. They __________ many different activities: watching the aurora borealis, __________ in the woods, observing animals and meeting Ana's friends. This part of the __________ is really amazing and is definetely worth a __________!

EXERCISE 3

Complete the following sentences:

1 • If I had known about that, I ______________________. (tell)

2 • If they go on holiday to Greece, they ______________________. (swim)

3 • If my father planted a cherry tree, we ______________________. (have fruit)

4 • I would not watch this movie, if I ______________________ you (be). It is too scary.

5 • If my brother and my sister listened to our parents, they ______________________ (not go on holiday on their own).

EPISODE 17

What are you saying?

EXERCISE 1

Complete the sentences according to the text:

1 • Lucie and Marc are going to meet Peter ______________________

2 • Peter's work at the museum is ______________________

3 • Lucie prefers art but Marc ______________________

4 • Both Helena and Peter have ______________________

EXERCISE 2

Read the blog entry again and complete the following table:

	TRUE	FALSE
Marc and Lucie had a hard time understanding people's accents.		
Visiting the museum was boring.		
Ottawa is the city with the most inhabitants in Canada.		
The Canadian Tulip Festival is very lively.		
Snowfalls can last until Spring.		

EXERCISE 3

Change the sentences using may:

1 • It is possible that I will celebrate my birthday in a nightclub.

---

2 • There's a chance my brother will win the tennis championship this weekend.

---

3 • Do you think I could come for Christmas?

---

4 • There is a possibility my dad will be promoted.

---

5 • There is a chance that I will finish, planting these flowers before lunch time.

EPISODE 18

Do You Speak . . . ?

EXERCISE 1

Listen to or read the dialogue again and choose the right answer:

1 • Today, Marc and Lucie are going to:
a. a bilingual school.
b. a French community.
c. an English meeting.

2 • In New Brunswick, people speak:
a. English.
b. French.
c. both English and French.

3 • At home, Laura speaks:
a. French.
b. English.
c. French and English.

4 • Laura studies in French:
a. physics and biology.
b. geography and history.
c. P.E.

5 • As a foreign language, Laura chose:
a. Spanish and Russian.
b. Chinese.
c. Spanish.

EXERCISE 2

Complete the text with the following words:
French/such/natural/stay/landscapes.

Laura and Marc enjoyed their ______________ in New Brunswick a lot. They learnt that people speak English and ______________ in this part of Canada. They also noted that it is a very ______________ area with a lot of nice different ______________: beaches, countryside and forests. It was a bit windy but ______________ a wonderful destination.

EXERCISE 3

Change the sentences in indirect speech:

1 • "It has been a long day."

His mother said ______________________________

2 • "We finished our book!"

My sisters said ______________________________

3 • "No! Don't drink this glass of wine!"

Her father said ______________________________

4 • "She may come back tomorrow."

We said ______________________________

5 • "Speak louder please."

The teacher asked him ______________________________

You are now ready to recap! Turn the page and **Check Your Skills!**

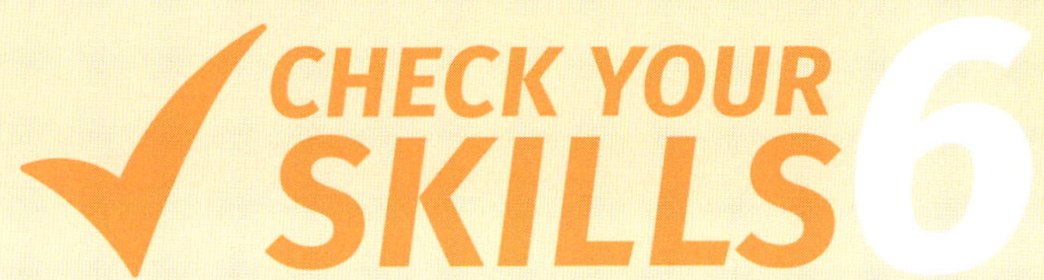

A Complete the sentences with the correct tenses:

1 • If I ____________ (be) you, I ____________ (hurry).

2 • If they ____________ (have) a new car, they ____________ (arrive) on time. Now it's too late!

3 • If he ____________ (study) more last week, he ____________ (succeed).

4 • If it ____________ (be) sunny, I ____________ (go) to the public garden.

5 • If we ____________ (know) he wasn't going to the wedding, we ____________ (invite) somebody else.

B Complete with still/already/ever/yet/too.

1 • He wanted to go with us ____________.

2 • My brother ____________ plays with his baby toys even though he is now 14!

3 • They haven't watched this movie ____________.

4 • Have you ____________ met my parents?

5 • My tennis coach has ____________ won a lot of tournaments.

C Change the sentences into indirect speech:

1 • I love my cat.

He said ....

2 • We are watching George Lucas's new movie.

They explained ....

3 • You will take your exam tomorrow at ten o'clock.

I said ....

4 • Don't be late!

You shouted ....

5 • I can swim for hours.

She thought ....

6 • She has left school recently.

They supposed ....

7 • We went to the restaurant yesterday evening.

She told me ....

D Write the following fractions in letters:

1 • 3/4 ....

2 • 3/5 ....

3 • 1/4 ....

Check your points!

(1 point for each correct sentence)

Exercise A: ________ points

Exercise B: ________ points

Exercise C: ________ points

Exercise D: ________ points

Total: ________ points

Between 15 and 20 points:

Well done! You can jump to the next episode! ☺

Between 10 and 15:

Pretty good! You may need to look back over some of the Tool Boxes.

Between 5 and 10:

Oops! I think you went too fast.

You should review some basic knowledge before going on.

Between 0 and 5:

Oops! You had better review episodes 16 to 18! Keep going!

EPISODE 19

A Ride to Cork

EXERCISE 1

Listen to or read the dialogue again and choose the right answer:

1 • Who are the main characters speaking in this dialogue?
a. Marc and Lucie.
b. Maureen and her dad.
c. Kilkenny and Cork.

2 • How did Maureen meet Marc and Lucie?
a. On a boat.
b. On the road.
c. On the Internet.

3 • Which sport does Maureen want Marc and Lucie to try?
a. Gaelic football.
b. Horse riding.
c. Stand-up paddle boarding.

4 • What journey will Maureen and her father do?
a. From Cork to Kilkenny.
b. From Dublin to Cork.
c. From Kilkenny to Cork.

5 • Where is Maureen's brother?
a. In town.
b. On a boat.
c. In a castle.

EXERCISE 2

Complete the text with the following words:
discover/Internet /traditional/stories/museum.

Maureen contacted Marc and Lucie on the ______________. She wanted to help them ______________ her county. Marc liked Maureen's brother's ______________ and visiting the Viking ______________. They tasted ______________ food and quite liked it!

EXERCISE 3

Complete the sentences with the following phrasal verbs (choose the right tense):
point out/make of/pick out/get rid of/look for.

1 • I ______________ my keys. Have you seen them?

2 • My sweater is very warm. It is ______________ wool.

3 • You need to ______________ these old clothes.

4 • My best friend ______________ a present for his girlfriend.

5 • Our maths teacher ______________ the most important parts of the chapter.

EPISODE **20**

Surfing Ireland!

EXERCISE 1

Listen to or read the dialogue again and link the sentences:

Lucie and Marc are in Dingle Bay	O	O	to observe dolphins properly.
Marc needs binoculars	O	O	because the waves are good.
Dingle Bay is a very touristy area	O	O	to take pictures of dolphins.
Dingle Bay is perfect for surfing	O	O	and this is not always good for the environment.
Lucie and Marc will take a boat	O	O	to watch animals and surfers.

EXERCISE 2

Read the blog entry again and complete the following table:

	TRUE	FALSE
Marc and Lucie went to see Fungie the dolphin.		
Liam performs every Saturday evening.		
Liam works in a pub.		
Liam's grandfather was interested in stories and legends.		
Lucie and Marc consider poetry to be a school subject.		

EXERCISE 3

Answer the following questions:

1 • Where did Lucie and Marc go in this episode?

---

2 • Who did they meet in Limerick?

---

3 • What did they watch in Dingle Bay?

---

4 • What is different about Liam's college?

Do you speak Gaelic?

EXERCISE 1

Listen to or read the dialogue again and complete the following table:

	TRUE	FALSE
The pub owner spoke to Marc and Lucie in English.		
Marc and Lucie visited Galway.		
Galway is a town with a lot of foreign students and tourists.		
Alana and Neil are cousins.		
Marc will go to the Clare Museum and Lucie to the Cliffs of Moher.		

EXERCISE 2

Choose the right answer:

1 • Marc and Neil went:
a. to the seaside.
b. to the Cliffs of Moher.
c. to the Clare Museum.

2 • Craggaunowen is:
a. a museum.
b. the reconstruction of a Celtic village.
c. a Bronze Age character.

3 • Marc and Lucie had:
a. a cold and rainy day.
b. beautiful weather.
c. snow and hail.

4 • Marc and Lucie finished their day with:
a. a nice dinner in a pub.
b. cakes and a hot drink at the tea room.
c. a beer and a burger.

EXERCISE 3

Change the sentences following the example:

Ex: They should go on holiday. => They should have gone on holiday.

1 • He should clean his father's car.

Yesterday, he should ________________

2 • They would do their homework.

Last weekend, they would ________________

3 • I could walk the dog.

This morning, I could ________________

4 • We may go camping in the mountains.

Last summer, we may ________________

5 • It must be warm enough to go to the lake.

Yesterday, I must ________________

You are now ready to recap! Turn the page and **Check Your Skills!**

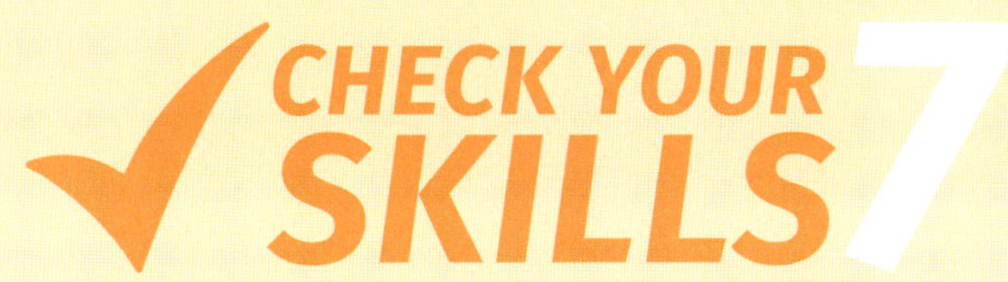

A **Complete the sentences with the following phrasal verbs: pick out/make up/set up/get on with/point out.**

1 • She wants the children to ______________ some new clothes.

2 • Twins usually ______________ well ______________ one another.

3 • Our mother always ______________ the importance of respecting others.

4 • My grandfather always ______________ new stories when we visit him!

5 • I ______________ a meeting to solve this problem.

B **Complete the sentences with the correct verbs following the example:**

Ex: My room was dirty. My mother made me clean it. (make/clean)

1 • I finished my essay early. That ______________. (allow/go out)

2 • My suitcases were very heavy. My boyfriend ______________ them. (help/carry)

3 • It's not very dangerous. ______________. (let/jump)

4 • They ______________ him. (persuade/watch this movie)

5 • He had no money to pay for a new car. That ______________ extra hours. (force/work)

C Change the following sentences into the past form:

1 • I should remove this poster from the wall.

---

2 • They may fight for this girl.

---

3 • He would prefer living in another city.

---

4 • You could bring a present for your aunt.

---

5 • We may know this person.

D Complete the text with a, the or Ø:

Yesterday, my cousin called me. He wanted to go to ________ swimming pool but I couldn't. I had ________ homework to do. I told him we could go this weekend but he couldn't. He was supposed to meet ________ friends and have ________ party on ________ beach.

Check your points!

(1 point for each correct sentence)

Exercise A: ________ points

Exercise B: ________ points

Exercise C: ________ points

Exercise D: ________ points

Total: ________ **points**

Between 15 and 20 points:

Well done! You can jump to the next episode! ☺

Between 10 and 15:

Pretty good! You may need to look back over some of the Tool Boxes.

Between 5 and 10:

Oops! I think you went too fast.

You should review some basic knowledge before going on.

Between 0 and 5:

Oops! You had better review episodes 19 to 21! Keep going!

EPISODE 22

A Step towards Tourism

EXERCISE 1

Listen to or read the dialogue again and complete the text with the following words: place/Causeway/flags/packed/Netherlands.

Lucie and Marc are in Northern Ireland. Today, they are visiting the Giant's ________________. It is a very touristy ________________. People take pictures and wave ________________. Marc and Lucie met people from the ________________, Australia, Nigeria and Sweden.

The place was stunning but ________________ with tourists.

EXERCISE 2

Read the blog entry again and link the two parts of the sentences:

Lucie and Marc visited	O	O	Catholics and Protestants.
They really were too many people	O	O	in the Titanic Museum.
The Troubles were between	O	O	the Giant's Causeway and the Titanic Museum.
At the Titanic Museum,	O	O	at the basalt columns site.
There are reconstructions of passenger cabins	O	O	you can learn about the ship but also get married.

EXERCISE 3

Choose the right answer:

1 • The basalt columns were made:
a. by a mythical creature.
b. by the crowd.
c. by a volcanic eruption.

2 • Lucie and Marc met:
a. only Irish people.
b. only foreigners.
c. both Irish people and foreigners.

3 • Lucie and Marc enjoyed:
a. visiting the Titanic Museum.
b. walking on the beach.
c. meeting tourists.

4 • In the Titanic Museum:
a. you can visit rooms similar to the ones on the ship.
b. you can have student parties.
c. you can buy a cruise ship.

5 • The Troubles is the name of:
a. the Titanic Museum.
b. the crowd of tourists in Irish tourist spots.
c. an armed conflict.

EPISODE 23

Commonwealth? Common Fun!

EXERCISE 1

Answer the following questions (write complete sentences):

1 • Who are Lucie and Marc meeting and where are they?

---

2 • What are they attending?

---

3 • What is the Commonwealth?

4 • What type of subjects do members discuss?

5 • Which countries are present this year? (quote at least three of them)

EXERCISE 2

Read the blog entry again and complete the following table:

	TRUE	FALSE
Lucie and Marc attended yesterday's discussions.		
Members mainly talked about peace in the world.		
New proposals are going to be submitted.		
Representatives of each country are elected by other teenagers.		
It's very gratifying to represent your country.		

EXERCISE 3

Change the sentences using be able to:

1 • I can break the window with a stone. (possibility)

2 • They can go to the post office. (past tense beginning with yesterday)

---

3 • You can take your driving test. (future tense beginning with tomorrow)

---

4 • We can help him tomorrow. (advice)

---

5 • She can sing better than that. (ability)

EPISODE 24

A Touch of Wales

EXERCISE 1

Listen to or read the dialogue again and choose the right answer:

1 • Where are Marc and Lucie?
a. In Wales.
b. On a sheep farm.
c. Back home.

2 • What do they visit next?
a. A ship.
b. The Isle of Anglesey.
c. A bridge.

3 • Who will introduce them to Welsh dancing?
a. Ally and Albert.
b. Malory
c. Ed and Molly.

4 • What will Lucie visit in Cardiff?
a. The Millennium Stadium.
b. The medieval castle.
c. Both the Millennium Stadium and the medieval castle.

5 • Who is Bob?
a. Their guide.
b. A sheep.
c. A dog.

EXERCISE 2

Complete the text with the following words:
three/landscapes/sheep/Wales/activities.

Marc and Lucie visited ____________ different places in ____________: Anglesey, Aberystwyth and Cardiff. They enjoyed all the ____________ they did. They just regretted they could not go to the Brecon Beacons National Park. The ____________ in Wales are really beautiful. So are the ____________!

EXERCISE 3

Change the sentences using have to:

1 • I probably need to go to the post office tomorrow. (doubt)

____

2 • I must believe in myself to succeed. (future)

____

3 • It's not necessary for him to finish his work. (unnecessary)

____

4 • They must clean the car before going on holiday. (yesterday)

____

5 • She must try harder! (regret)

____

You are now ready to recap! Turn the page and **Check Your Skills!**

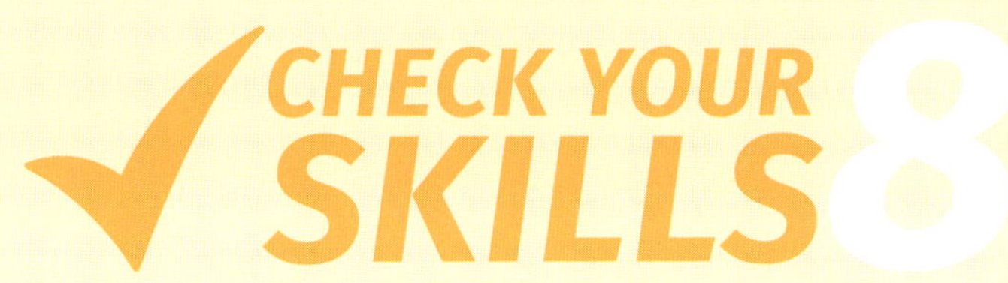

A **Complete the sentences with the following words: would like... to/can't wait to/will have to/ be expecting/want to.**

1 • I'm so excited. I love him so much. I ______________ watch this actor's new movie.

2 • She ______________ her dad to come with her.

3 • They ______________ us ______________ help them. They never do anything.

4 • There's almost no more bread at the bakery. They ______________ go now if they want some.

5 • You ______________ ______________ me ______________ take the car to the garage.

B **Complete the sentences with the following words: asked... not to/prefers to/will be ordered not to/is ordering... to/asked... to.**

1 • He ______________ go to the doctor rather than to the dentist.

2 • We ______________ them ______________ hurry up.

3 • The director ______________ him ______________ come quickly.

4 • I ______________ you ______________ shout so loud.

5 • You ______________ go that way.

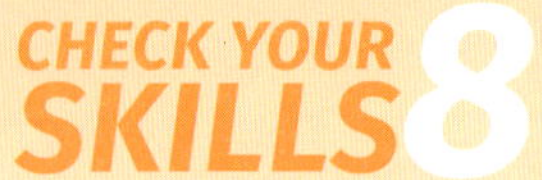

C Complete the sentences using to be able to:

I can stay by the seaside => I am able to stay by the seaside.

1. Yesterday, I ______________ go to the swimming pool.
2. Next week, they ______________ camp in the mountains.
3. If it is sunny, we ______________ go to the beach. But the weather forecast is not optimistic.
4. You ______________ play tennis for three hours and you're still not tired.
5. If she had worked harder, she ______________ to succeed.

D Complete the sentences with have to:

1 • It was late. She ______________ . (hurry).

2 • They ______________ for hours to learn this poem. (work)

3 • They ______________ carefully tomorrow. (listen)

4 • She will leave in a minute. They ______________ her right now. (see)

5 • Our computer was broken. We ______________ another one. (buy)

Check your points!

(1 point for each correct sentence)

Exercise A: ______ points

Exercise B: ______ points

Exercise C: ______ points

Exercise D: ______ points

Total: ______ **points**

Between 15 and 20 points:

Well done! You can jump to the next episode! ☺

Between 10 and 15:

Pretty good! You may need to look back over some of the Tool Boxes.

Between 5 and 10:

Oops! I think you went too fast.

You should review some basic knowledge before going on.

Between 0 and 5:

Oops! You had better review episodes 22 to 24! Keep going!

EPISODE
25

Time to Go Home

EXERCISE 1

Listen to or read the dialogue again and complete the table:

	TRUE	FALSE
This episode is the last one.		
Marc and Lucie want to spend time with their friends and family.		
The blog received a lot of bad comments.		
Marc took loads of pictures.		
Marc does not want to travel with Lucie anymore.		
Marc forgot his suitcase at the hotel.		

EXERCISE 2

Complete the following sentences:

1 • What Lucie really loved ....

2 • People liked reading the blog to ....

3 • Lucie was happy to share ....

4 • One of the first things Marc wants to do is ....

....

5 • At the end of the dialogue, it is time to ....

EXERCISE 3

Complete the text with the following words:
home/positive/travel/happy/posts/something.

Lucie and Marc were very ______________ to write this blog and moved by readers' ______________ reactions. They are encouraging people to ______________, even if the destination is close to their ______________. There is always ______________ new to discover. They also want to keep on travelling and will certainly write more ______________ on their blog.

EXERCISE 4

Link the two parts of the sentences:

Marc and Lucie first	O	O	all the positive reactions to their blog.
Their blog contains	O	O	is one of Marc and Lucie's projects.
They really appreciated	O	O	write a blog during their next trip.
A new trip	O	O	texts, pictures and paintings.
They will certainly	O	O	visited African countries.

Answers

EPISODE 1: A New Hope!

EXERCISE 1

	T	F
Lucie and Marc won an English-speaking countries world tour.	X	
Lucie and Marc know about their programme.		X
Marc wants to taste hamburgers.	X	
Lucie does not want to go.		X
Marc is happy about writing a blog.	X	

EXERCISE 2

1 • Marc is from Germany.
2 • Lucie is 19 years old.
3 • Marc and Lucie will visit English speaking countries.
4 • Marc and Lucie will post texts, pictures and paintings on their blog.
5 • Yes, she is very talented.

EXERCISE 3

1 • Marc and Lucie are friends.
2 • Do you like discovering new places?
3 • What types of monuments do you like visiting?
4 • Marc and Lucie met last year in Egypt.
5 • The blog will contain texts and pictures.

EPISODE 2: Road Trip

EXERCISE 1

1 • a. (Lucie and Marc will leave in February.)
2 • a. (Lucie and Marc will first visit Nigeria.)
3 • c. (The Tasmanian Devil is an animal.)
4 • a. (It's in a movie).
5 • b. (Lucie knows about Nunavut because it's a place famous for Native Indian art.)
6 • c. (They will surf).
7 • c. (Off the coasts of Ireland and the UK.)

EXERCISE 2

	T	F
The trip will be very short.		X
Marc is very excited to go to Australia.	X	
Marc wants to learn an African language.		X
Lucie does not like Nunavut art.		X
Lucie and Marc think all the places will be interesting to visit.	X	

EXERCISE 3

Marc and Lucie are so **happy**. They received the programme for their trip. They will visit many places in Africa, Australia, New Zealand, North **America** and the British Isles. Their **favourite** places will certainly be Cairns (for Marc) and Nunavut (for Lucie). They like nature and art but also **discovering** new things, like languages.

EPISODE 3: What Does it Take to Tour the World?

EXERCISE 1

1 • Marc is packing his bag.
2 • No, Lucie thinks Marc is not organised.
3 • Mark put his clothes on his bed.
4 • Mark's mobile phone is on the floor, behind the door.
5 • Mark's passport is on his desk.
6 • Yes, Lucie's bag is ready.

EXERCISE 2

1 • Marc's suitcase is really heavy.
2 • Lucie hopes she won't feel home-sick.

3 • Lucie went to Milan a few years ago.
4 • Marc decided to take a German key ring.
5 • Their first destination is Nigeria.

EXERCISE 3

1 • a. (Lucie did not forget her cuddly toy.)
2 • b. (Lucie wants to post pictures on their blog regularly.)
3 • a. (Lucie's lucky charm is a rubber.)
4 • a. (Marc's lucky charm is a key ring.)

CHECK YOUR SKILLS 1

A. Complete the sentences with the following words: can/mustn't/goes/will/went.

1 • Tom **will** go to the swimming pool next Saturday.
2 • Clara **went** to school by bike yesterday.
3 • Peter **goes** to the public garden with his dog every Sunday.
4 • I **can** run very fast.
5 • You **mustn't** cross the street without looking.

B. Complete the sentences with the following words: What/Where/When/Who/How/Why.

1 • **When** is your birthday?
2 • **What** will you do next Monday?
3 • **Why** are you crying?
4 • **How** are you?
5 • **Where** did you buy this book?

C. Make up four sentences with exclamatory words using the adjective "beautiful" and the noun "castle".

1 • What a beautiful castle!
2 • This is such a beautiful castle!
3 • How beautiful this castle is!
4 • This castle is so beautiful!

D. Complete with the right personal pronoun

1 • **My** brother said I am not organised.
2 • **He/She** wants to go to the swimming pool.
3 • This dog is wandering in the street. Maybe **it** is lost.
4 • My mother likes **her** job a lot.
5 • My sister and her boyfriend are on holiday. **They** are in Malawi.

E. Complete the sentences with the following words: so much/so many/how much/many/too many.

1 • **How much** is this T-shirt?
2 • There were **so many** people at that concert that we could not dance!
3 • **Many** students work to earn money.
4 • Don't put **so much** water in your bath!
5 • There are **too many** cars on the road! We will be late!

F. Complete the sentences in a logical way:

1 • **The cleverest** boy of the class is Leo.
2 • **The nicest** cat on Earth is my cat!
3 • Wow! This movie is **as interesting as** the one I watched last week.
4 • A mouse is **smaller than** a cat
5 • This place is **less large than** the other one.
6 • Today, I am **less cheerful than** I was yesterday.

G. Complete with the following words: anywhere/anything/somebody/nowhere/nobody/something.

1 • **Somebody** is knocking at the door.
2 • Did you leave **anything** at school?
3 • **Nobody** knows where he is.
4 • I cannot find my keys **anywhere**.
5 • I need **something** to fix this.
6 • We have **nowhere** to go. All the hotels are full.

Answers

H. Make up sentences with the following words:

1 • My father's wallet is on the table.
2 • The page of the book is torn.
3 • Your grand-mother's trees are tall.
4 • The album of the year is great.

EPISODE 4: Connected Cocoa

EXERCISE 1

1 • a. (Dunjuma grows cocoa trees.)
2 • c. (Dunjuma has worked with his father for 4.)
3 • b. (Dunjuma sells his cocoa in Europe.)
4 • a. (Dunjuma uses an electric car.)

EXERCISE 2.

	T	F
There are several official languages in Nigeria.	X	
There is a rainy and a dry season in Nigeria.	X	
You can find cocoa, banana and mango trees in Nigeria.	X	
Cocoa beans must be dried before people put them into big bags.	X	
Dunjuma's cocoa beans are exported by plane.		X

EXERCISE 3

1 • Marc and Lucie ate marvellous mango fruit.
2 • Dunjuma has an eco-friendly attitude.
3 • Cocoa beans travel to Europe by boat.
4 • Lagos is the biggest city in Nigeria.
5 • In Nigeria, people speak English, Haoussa, Yoruba and Igbo.

EPISODE 5: South Africa Past and Future

EXERCISE 1

Lucie and Marc visited Bo-Kaap in **South Africa/Cape Town**. Nelson showed them **painted** houses. Nelson has a lot of **friends** there. There is a museum of slavery because many **slaves** lived there some **centuries** ago. Now, the area is **recognised** as a National Heritage Site.

EXERCISE 2

1 • I could understand the whole song.
2 • Marc could hear the sound of a river.
3 • We could see beautiful stars in the sky.
4. • Lucie could taste so many vegetables in her soup.
5 • They could feel the tension between their parents.

EXERCISE 3.

	T	F
Lucie put pictures of Bo-Kaap on the blog.	X	
Lucie and Marc were very moved by the history of Bo-Kaap.	X	
Bo-Kaap is a modern place.		X
Marc and Lucie went to the jungle.		X
Part of the population is poor and lives in poor housing conditions.	X	

EPISODE 6: A Full-Time Job

EXERCISE 1

1 • Kilimanjaro is more than 5,500 metres high.
2 • Kofi is a ranger who protects wild animals.
3 • In the 1990's, the National Park became a real swamp.

4 • The National Park has been a reserve since the 1970's.

5 • Kofi works at the park because he loves animals.

EXERCISE 2

Marc and Lucie **visited** a Maasai village. They met **teenagers** and listened to stories under a starlit **sky**. They understood that most teenagers are **concerned** with the same things: love, **friendship** and the future (and the future of the planet!).

EXERCISE 3

1 • b. (Lucie and Marc watched wild animals.)

2 • a. (Kofi took them to a traditional African village.)

3 • a. (Marc and Lucie could listen to traditional stories.)

4 • b. (African teenagers were surprised to see Lucie and Marc.)

5 • c. (They spoke with African teenagers and realised they have a lot in common.)

✓ CHECK YOUR SKILLS 2

A. Complete the sentences with the preterite:

1 • My parents **went** to Venice for their wedding anniversary four years ago.

2 • Mr Wilson **tried** to play golf more often than last year.

3 • When I **was** young, my favourite teacher **was** Mrs Albert.

4 • I **had** a very nice birthday party two weeks ago.

B. the sentences with the present perfect:

1 • I **have waited** for this letter for three days.

2 • He **has spoken** on the phone with his friends for one hour!

3 • The children **have played** football for hours.

4 • I **have spent** time at the swimming pool this morning.

C. Choose between preterite and present perfect:

1 • Last week, I **went** to my best friend's birthday party.

2 • She **has lived** in New York for 4 years. She now lives in Dubai.

3 • Since I was born, I **have loved** listening to music.

4 • I **studied** Japanese 6 years ago.

D. Choose between "for" and "since":

1 • I have played tennis **for** 3 years.

2 • This restaurant has been here **for** a long time.

3 • A lot of rain has fallen **since** the beginning of the week.

4 • This restaurant has been here **since** 2002.

E. Choose between "a few" or "a little":

1 • I only have **a little** money in my purse.

2 • **A few** children are playing in the playground.

3 • Could you give me **a little** milk?

4 • She has **a few** problems to solve.

EPISODE 7: Native Art

EXERCISE 1

1 • Natural pigments take long to prepare, which is why some artists use industrial ones.

2 • Instead of painting some people prefer to make sculptures.

3 • Unless you meet the artists, you cannot know if they use natural pigments.

4 • In order to see beautiful sculptures, Lucie and Marc have to go to the Parklands.

5 • If you like art, you can go to the Adelaide Festival of Arts.

Answers

EXERCISE 2

Lucie and Marc had a wonderful **evening**. In town they met a group of young **Australians** and they went to the **beach** with them. They **discussed** The Aboriginal situation and sang **traditional** songs while watching the sunset.

EXERCISE 3

	T	F
Marc and Lucie visited only some of the exhibits.		X
They met a group of young Australians in the Parklands.	X	
All the young people were native Australians.		X
European settlers were nice to Aborigines.		X
Lucie and Marc enjoyed their evening on the sand a lot.	X	

EPISODE 8: OK Coral!

EXERCISE 1

1 • Lucie and Marc are meeting Archie, a volunteer who protects the Great Barrier Reef.
2 • The Foundation visits schools to alert children to marine pollution.
3 • The Foundation wants people to protect the Great Barrier Reef.
4 • The children from a nearby school cleaned all the plastic garbage from the beach.
5 • Lucie and Marc are going scuba diving to admire the Great Barrier Reef.

EXERCISE 2

Marc and Lucie **loved** scuba diving with Archie. The Great Barrier Reef is so **colourful**. Then, they went to the Outback, a very **dry** and unpopulated area in Central Australia. They met **young** students who work on **farms** during their gap year.

EXERCISE 3

1 • I **could have gone** to the cinema yesterday but I had exams.
2 • You **should have watched** this movie. It was really great.
3 • My brother **could have had more fun** playing another sport. He really didn't like this one.
4 • We **should have paid more attention** to this problem. It is too late to fix it now.

EPISODE 9: Weird Animals!

EXERCISE1

	T	F
Tasmania is smaller than Australia.	X	
Paula works for the University of Australia.		X
Lucie needs her camera.	X	
Wombats eat meat.		X
Wombats are the only protected animals in Tasmania.		X

EXERCISE 2

1 • a. (Paula went to Sydney to sail from Sydney to Tasmania.)
2 • c. (Paula's husband is crazy about car races, wich is why he goes to a car race every year.)
3 • b. (In Australia, summer holidays take place in December/January because people don't live in the Northern Hemisphere.)
4 • b. (Australian schoolchildren wear uniforms.)
5 • c. (Marc would love to go to school in Australia because he could give up maths.)

EXERCISE 3

1 • For three years, I have played rugby every Wednesday.

2 • I went to the swimming pool last Sunday.
3 • Yesterday, I watched horror movies.
4 • Since I was young, I have eaten ice cream.
5 • I have painted/painted my house for hours.

CHECK YOUR SKILLS 3

A. Complete the sentences with the following words: because of/however/in order to/ on the contrary/therefore.

1 • I went to the park this afternoon to meet my friends. **However** I could not find them.
2 • "You don't like gardening?" "**On the contrary**, I love it."
3 • He did not work hard enough. **Therefore**, he failed his English exam.
4 • **In order to** get there on time, we'll take the bus.
5 • **Because of** the noise, I could not hear what she said.

B. Complete the sentences with the following words: while/but/in front of/behind/even if.

1 • **While** sleeping, I dreamt about my next holiday.
2 • Your school bag? You can't see it from here. It is just **behind** the door!
3 • I need to go to the doctor **but** I don't have time today...
4 • Can't you see it? It's just **in front of** you, on the table.
5 • **Even if** you ask me, I won't tell you.

C. Make up sentences that match the drawing, based in this example:

1. The little girl wants her dog to jump.
2. They want her to ride this bike.
3. She wants him to read/take this book.
4. The girls don't want the boy to use their ball/to play with them.
5. The woman wants the other woman to come in.

D. Complete with the correct tense: simple present/simple past/present perfect.

1 • Yesterday I **went** to the cinema with my best friend.
2 • My uncle **has played** tennis since he was 6 years old.
3 • Children usually **like** eating chocolate biscuits.
4 • My parents and I **visited** Ireland 6 years ago.
5 • France **has been** part of the European Union for years.

EPISODE 10: Let's score!

EXERCISE 1

Lucie and Marc met Kasia and Ted. Kasia is a rugby player and Ted is a cricket player. These sports are very popular in their country. It's not common for girls to play rugby but more and more are doing so. Marc does not play sports but plays video games.

EXERCISE 2

1 • b. (Lucie and Marc watched the match with Ted.)
2 • b. (the following day, Kasia and Marc went to the beach.)
3 • b. (The teenagers had fun paddling.)
4 • a. (also tasted a traditional pastry.)

EXERCISE 3

1 • My brother feels like going to the beach.
2 • My best friend feels like learning Italian.
3 • I feel like traveling to/visiting Mexico.
4 • They feel like watching this movie.

Answers

EPISODE 11:
Welcome to New Zealand!

EXERCISE1

	T	F
Anahera and Tamati both speak Maori.	X	
The Maori language is spoken only in New Zealand.		X
The Maori language is spoken only in a family context.		X
In the past, Maori used to be an oral language.	X	
Hangi is a traditional dance.		X

EXERCISE 2

1 • Marc and Lucie went to Massey University to meet a professor, Prof. Longworth.

2 • Courses on Maori culture are for everybody, Maori and non-Maori people.

3 • An automatic translator is included in Prof. Longworth's projects.

4 • Marc tried to translate swear words.

EXERCISE 3

1 • The Maori language can be learnt at university.

2 • Children are told Maori legends by older people./Maori Legends are told to children by older people.

3 • Traditional songs are not often sung by young people.

4 • The blog post has to be written before ten o'clock (by Lucie and Marc).

EPISODE 12:
Lord of the Cinema!

EXERCISE 1

1 • a. (The name 'Matamata' comes from an animal.)

2 • c. (Marc is happy because he is glad to visit Matamata and the Hobbit village.)

3 • c. (The cinema industry in New Zealand is a real advantage for the country).

4 • b. (You need a lot of people to shoot a movie: actors, technicians and makeup artists.)

5 • a. (Lucie thinks cinema is important for the area because it adds magic.)

EXERCISE 2

1 • Lucie and Marc loved the Matamata area.

2 • Matamata has a lot more to offer than just the visit to the Hobbit village.

3 • Not far away, there is a small town with restaurants and places to visit.

4 • In the autumn, the countryside is colourful and packed with animals.

5 • Marc and Lucie encourage you to come and visit the Matamata area.

EXERCISE 3

Marc absolutely wanted to visit Matamata because he is a big fan of Lord of the Rings. The movie was shot there. He was so happy to celebrate his birthday there. Lucie brought a cupcake! They both liked the area a lot. It is natural and beautiful in the autumn.

CHECK YOUR SKILLS 4

A. Complete the sentences with "in", "on", "to" or "from"

1 • My neighbours are going on holiday in July.

2 • My brother will move to Boston next September.

3 • On Sundays, there is no school!

4 • Salvatore? He is in Venezuela at the moment.

5 • Elizabeth I reigned in the 16th century.

B. Change these active sentences into passive sentences:

1 • Basketball is played by a lot of people.

2 • America was discovered by Christopher Columbus.
3 • The whole house has been cleaned (by me).
4 • This house was built by Mr Simpson in 1956.
5 • Peter has been hit by Clara.

C. Transform these active sentences into passive sentences:

1 • The problem could be understood by only two people.
2 • My bike must be repaired by my dad.
3 • The computer would be used by the whole class.
4 • The cake should be made before tomorrow (by us).
5 • This book can be exchanged by Peter.

D. Complete the sentences:

1 • I think you will sleep tomorrow.
2 • She guessed you would like to listen to music.
3 • My uncle supposed his nephew would be happy to play tennis.
4 • Marc said he would be interested in visiting Matamata.
5 • They say the woman will work for a few more hours.

EPISODE 13: Flea Market Day

EXERCISE1	T	F
Portland is situated on the East Coast.		X
Marc went to a flea market with his parents when he was 12.	X	
Lucie likes the lamp.	X	
Portland is one of the greenest cities in the US.	X	
Lucie wants to buy a necklace.		X

EXERCISE 2

1 • In Portland, you can use the tram to go to work.
2 • They organise flea markets to encourage people to re-use things.
3 • Portland won two prizes for being environmentally-friendly.
4 • Marc didn't want to go to a vegan restaurant because he likes meat too much.
5 • In the end, Marc liked vegan food.

EXERCISE 3

Here are some possible answers:

1 • She wonders when her boyfriend is coming.
2 • They don't know what to do/what they can do.
3 • He wants to know where the station is.
4 • She asks him who this boy is.
5 • She wonders whose keys these are.

EPISODE 14: Middle of Nowhere

EXERCISE 1

1 • c. (Lucie would like to visit museums.)
2 • b. (Aisling lives on a farm.)
3 • a. (Marc wants to go to the national park.)
4 • b. (Aisling's farm is far from a big town.)
5 • a. (Aisling comes back from school on weekends.)

EXERCISE 2

Lucie and Marc were very impressed by the Midwest region. They visited large open spaces, an Indian reserve and Roosevelt National Park. They also went to South Dakota and had a look at the Mount Rushmore sculptures. They enjoyed their stay with Aishling and also getting away from the big cities.

EXERCISE 3

1 • I'd rather go to the swimming pool than to school.

Answers

2 • Whether you're interested or not, I will tell you about my day!
3 • I would like to take either my bike or the bus to go to the cinema.
4 • Lucie plans to visit Berlin whether Marc wants to or not.
5 • It is so cold today that they'd better take their scarves.

EPISODE 15: A Taste of New Orleans!

EXERCISE1.

	T	F
Tom has been living in New Orleans for a very long time.		X
Tom likes the city a lot.	X	
Marc is really keen on visiting the Voodoo Museum.		X
Lucie wants to visit a plantation.		X
Marc thinks gumbo is a dance.	X	
Lucie knows what gumbo is.	X	

EXERCISE 2

1 • Lucie and Marc visited the French Quarter.
2 • The Cajuns are people with a French origin.
3 • You can tour the Mississippi on steamboats.
4 • Lucie and Marc visited the "big house" and the slave quarter.
5 • They felt sad on the plantation.

EXERCISE 3

1 • Yesterday, my friend and I went to the flea market.
2 • I thought he had finished his homework before he played football.
3 • We have been planning this trip for many years. We are so disappointed it's cancelled.
4 • My uncle have played football all his life. He's the best.
5 • She remembered she had visited this place when she was young.

CHECK YOUR SKILLS 5

A. Complete the following sentences with an indirect question:

1 • She is wondering who is singing in the street
2 • I'm asking you when you bought this new wallet.
3 • They are wondering where their cousin's new house is.
4 • You are asking her why I am late.
5 • He wants to know how James is.

B. Transform the sentences using " 'd rather" or " 'd better":

1. You'd better listen to your parents!
2. I'd rather go to the mountains on holiday.
3. If they had the choice, they'd rather choose the blue one.
4. She'd better read this new novel.
5. She'd better not tell them about it.

C. Complete the following sentences with "whether/or" or "either/or":

1. Whether you revised or not, I'm sure you will succeed.
2. Whether he wants to or not, he will try to solve this problem.
3. I can take either meat or fish, I don't mind.
4. Whether you choose this house or the other one, we will move to a fantastic neighbourhood.
5. They can pick you up at the airport either by car or by taxi.

D. Complete the sentences with the correct tense (preterite, present perfect simple, present perfect continuous or past perfect):

1. My cousin and I participated in a music festival.
2. She has studied Japanese for several weeks, and she loves it.
3. They thought we had written to our grandparents before they came back from the seaside.
4. He worked on this essay for hours yesterday.
5. I remembered you had watched this movie before we met.

EPISODE 16: Please Meet . . .

EXERCISE 1

1 • c. (They are walking to watch the aurora borealis.)
2 • a. (Lucie especially appreciates silence.)
3 • a. (They are going to camp.)
4 • c. (He wants to fish in the river.)
5 • b. (It is a savage legendary creature.)

EXERCISE 2

Ana took Lucie and Marc to the Far North, in Canada. They enjoyed many different activities: watching the aurora borealis, hiking in the woods, observing animals and meeting Ana's friends. This part of the world is really amazing and is definitely worth a visit!

EXERCISE 3

1 • If I had known about that, I would have told you/him/her/them.
2 • If they go on holiday to Greece, they will swim.
3 • If my father planted a cherry tree, we would have fruit.
4 • I would not watch this movie, if I were/was you. It is too scary.
5 • If my brother and my sister listened to our parents, they would not go on holiday on their own.

EPISODE 17: What are you saying?

EXERCISE 1

1 • Lucie and Marc are going to meet Peter at the science museum.
2 • Peter's work at the museum is his student job.
3 • Lucie prefers art but Marc loves all kinds of science.
4 • Both Helena and Peter have a strong accent when they speak English.

EXERCISE 2

	T	F
Marc and Lucie had a hard time understanding people's accents.	X	
Visiting the museum was boring.		X
Ottawa is the city with the most inhabitants in Canada.		X
The Canadian Tulip Festival is very lively.	X	
Snowfalls can last until Spring.	X	

EXERCISE 3

1 • I may celebrate my birthday in a nightclub.
2 • My brother may win the tennis championship this weekend.
3 • May I come for Christmas?
4 • My dad may be promoted.
5 • I may finish planting these flowers before lunch time.

Answers

EPISODE 18: Do You Speak . . . ?

EXERCISE 1

1 • a. (Today, Marc and Lucie are going to a bilingual school.)
2 • c. (In New Brunswick, people speak both English and French.)
3 • b. (At home, Laura speaks English.)
4 • b. (Laura studies geography and history in French.)
5 • c. (As a foreign language, Laura chose Spanish.)

EXERCISE 2

Laura and Marc enjoyed their **stay** in New Brunswick a lot. They learnt that people speak English and **French** in this part of Canada. They also noted that it is a very **natural** area with a lot of nice different **landscapes**: beaches, countryside and forests. It was a bit windy but **such** a wonderful destination.

EXERCISE 3

1 • His mother said it had been a long day.
2 • My sisters said they had finished their book.
3 • Her father said not to drink that glass of wine.
4 • We said she might come back tomorrow.
5 • The teacher asked him to speak louder.

✓ CHECK YOUR SKILLS 6

A. Complete the sentences with the correct tenses:

1 • If I **were** you, I **would** hurry.
2 • If they **had had** a new car, they **would have arrived** on time. Now it's too late!
3 • If he **had studied** more last week, he **would have succeeded**.
4 • If it **is** sunny, I **will go** to the public garden.
5 • If we **had known** he wasn't going to the wedding, we **would have invited** somebody else.

B. Complete with: still/already/ever/yet/too.

1 • He wanted to go with us **too**.
2 • My brother **still** plays with his baby toys even though is now 14!
3 • They haven't watched this movie **yet**.
4 • Have you **ever** met my parents?
5 • My tennis coach has **already** won a lot of tournaments.

C. Change the sentences into indirect speech:

1 • He said that he loved his cat.
2 • They explained that they were watching George Lucas's new movie.
3 • I said he/she/they would take his/her/their exam tomorrow at ten o'clock.
4 • You shouted (at us) not to be late.
5 • She thought she could swim for hours.
6 • They supposed she had left school recently.
7 • She told me they had gone/been to the restaurant yesterday evening.

D. Write the following fractions in letters:

1 • Three quarters.
2 • Three-fifths.
3 • One quarter/A quarter.

EPISODE 19: A Ride to Cork

EXERCISE 1

1 • b. (The main characters speaking in this dialogue are Maureen and her dad.)
2 • c. (Maureen met Marc and Lucie on the Internet.)
3 • a. (Maureen wants Marc and Lucie to try Gaelic football.)
4 • c. (Maureen and her father drive from Kilkenny to Cork.)
5 • b. (Maureen's brother is on a boat.)

EXERCISE 2

Maureen contacted Marc and Lucie on the **Internet**. She wanted to help them **discover** her county. Marc liked Maureen's brother's **stories** and visiting the Viking **museum**. They tasted **traditional** food and quite liked it!

EXERCISE 3

1 • I **am looking** for my keys. Have you seen them?
2 • My sweater is very warm. It is **made of** wool.
3 • You need to **get rid of** these old clothes.
4 • My best friend **picked out** a present for his girlfriend.
5 • Our maths teacher **is pointing out** the most important parts of the chapter.

EPISODE 20: Surfing Ireland!

EXERCISE 1

1 • Lucie and Marc are in Dingle Bay to take pictures of dolphins.
2 • Marc needs binoculars to watch animals and surfers.
3 • Dingle Bay is a very touristy area and this is not always good for the environment.
4 • Dingle Bay is perfect for surfing because the waves are good.
5 • Lucie and Marc will take a boat to observe dolphins properly.

EXERCISE 2

	T	F
Marc and Lucie went to Fungie.		X
Liam performs every Saturday evening.	X	
Liam works in a pub.		X
Liam's grandfather was interested in stories and legends.	X	
Lucie and Marc consider poetry to be a school subject.	X	

EXERCISE 3

1 • Lucie and Marc went to southern Ireland in this episode.
2 • They met Liam in Limerick.
3 • They watched dolphins in Dingle Bay.
4 • Liam likes writing poetry.

EPISODE 21: Do you speak Gaelic?

EXERCISE1

	T	F
The pub owner spoke to Marc and Lucie in English.		X
Marc and Lucie visited Galway.	X	
Galway is a town with a lot of foreign students and tourists.	X	
Alana and Neil are cousins.		X
Marc will go to the Clare Museum and Lucie to the Cliffs of Moher.		X

EXERCISE 2

1 • b. (Marc and Neil went to the Cliffs of Moher.)
2 • b. (is the reconstruction of a Celtic village.)
3 • a. (Marc and Lucie had a cold and rainy day.)
4 • b. (Marc and Lucie finished their day with cakes and a hot drink at the tea room.)

EXERCISE 3

1 • Yesterday, he should have cleaned his father's car.
2 • Last week-end, they would have done their homework.
3 • This morning, i could have walked the dog.
4 • Last summer, we may have gone camping in the mountains.
5 • Yesterday, it must have been warm enough to go to the lake.

Answers

✓ CHECK YOUR SKILLS 7

A. Complete the sentences with the following phrasal verbs: pick out/make up/set up/get on with/ point out.

1 • She wants the children to **pick out** some new clothes.

2 • Twins usually **get on** well **with** one another.

3 • Our mother always **points out** the importance of respecting others.

4 • My grandfather always **makes up** new stories when we visit him!

5 • I **set up** a meeting to solve this problem.

B. Complete the sentences with the correct verbs:

1 • I finished my essay early. That **allowed me to go out**.

2 • My suitcases were very heavy. My boyfriend **helped me to carry** them.

3 • It's not very dangerous. **Let me jump**.

4 • They **persuaded him to watch this movie**.

5 • He had no money to pay for a new car. That **forced him to work** extra hours.

C. Change the following sentences into past form:

1 • I should have removed this poster from the wall.

2 • They may have fought for this girl.

3 • He would have preferred living in another city.

4 • You could have brought a present for your aunt.

5 • We may have known this person.

D. Complete the text with "a", "the" or Ø:

Yesterday, my cousin called me. He wanted to go to **the** swimming pool but I couldn't. I had **Ø** homework to do. I told him we could go this weekend but he couldn't. He was supposed to meet **Ø** friends and have **a** party on **the** beach.

EPISODE 22: A Step towards Tourism

EXERCISE 1

Lucie and Marc are in Northern Ireland. Today, they are visiting the Giant's **Causeway**. It is a very touristic **place**. People take pictures and wave **flags**. Marc and Lucie met people from the **Netherlands**, Australia, Nigeria and Sweden. The place was stunning but touristy.

EXERCISE 2

1 • Lucie and Marc visited the Giant's Causeway and the Titanic Museum.

2 • They really were too many people at the basalt columns site.

3 • The Troubles were between Catholics and Protestants.

4 • At the Titanic Museum, you can learn about the boat but also get married.

5 • There are reconstructions of passenger cabins in the Titanic Museum.

EXERCISE 3

1 • c. (The basalt columns were made by a volcanic eruption.)

2 • c. (Lucie and Marc met both Irish people and foreigners.)

3 • a. (Lucie and Marc enjoyed visiting the Titanic Museum.)

4 • a. (In the Titanic Museum, you can visit rooms similar to the ones on the ship.)

5 • c. (The Troubles is the name of an armed conflict.)

EPISODE 23: Commonwealth? Common Fun!

EXERCISE 1

1 • Lucie and Marc are meeting Alister on the Isle of Man.

2 • They are attending the Commonwealth of Youth.

3 • The Commonwealth is a political association of fifty-three countries.

4 • They discuss ecology or immigration.

5 • Botswana, Uganda, Malaysia, Sri Lanka, Malta and Singapore.

EXERCISE 2

	T	F
Lucie and Marc attended yesterday's discussions.		X
Members mainly talked about peace in the world.		X
New proposals are going to be submitted.	X	
Representatives of each country are elected by other teenagers.	X	
It's very gratifying to represent your country.	X	

EXERCISE 3

1 • I may be able to break the window with a stone.

2 • Yesterday, they were able to go to the post office.

3 • Tomorrow, you will be able to take your driving test.

4 • We should be able to help him tomorrow.

5 • She must be able to sing better than that.

EPISODE 24: A Touch of Wales

EXERCISE 1

1 • a. (Marc and Lucie are in Wales).

2 • b. (The Isle of Anglesey is their next visit).

3 • c. (Ed and Molly will introduce them to Welsh dancing).

4 • b. (Lucie will visit the medieval castle in Cardiff).

5 • b. (Bob is a sheep).

EXERCISE 2

Marc and Lucie visited **three** different places in **Wales**: Anglesey, Aberystwyth and Cardiff. They enjoyed all the **activities** they did. They just regretted they could not go to the Brecon Beacons National Park. The landscapes in Wales are really beautiful. So are the **sheep**!

EXERCISE 3

1 • I may have to go to the post office tomorrow.

2 • I will have to believe in myself to succeed.

3 • He doesn't have to finish his work.

4 • Yesterday, they had to clean the car before going on holiday.

5 • She should have tried harder!

CHECK YOUR SKILLS 8

A. Complete the sentences with the following words: would like... to/can't wait to/will have to/be expecting/want to.

1 • I'm so excited. I love him so much. I **can't wait to** watch this actor's new movie.

2 • She **would like** her dad to come with her.

3 • They **want** us **to** help them. They never do anything.

4 • There's almost no more bread at the bakery. They **have to** go now if they want some.

5 • You **were expecting** me **to** take the car to the garage.

B. Complete the sentences with the following words:

1 • He **prefers to** go to the doctor rather than to the dentist.

2 • We **asked** them **to** hurry up.

Answers

3 • The director **is ordering** him **to** come quickly.
4 • I **asked** you **not** to shout so loud.
5 • You **will be ordered not to** go that way.

C. Complete the sentences using "to be able to":

1 • Yesterday, I was able to go to the swimming pool.
2 • Next week, they will be able to camp in the mountains.
3 • If it is sunny, we may be able to go to the beach.
4 • You have been able to play tennis for three hours and you're still not tired.
5 • If she had worked harder, she would have been able to succeed.

D. Complete the sentences with "have to":

1 • It was late. She **had to** hurry.
2 • They **had to work** for hours to learn this poem.
3 • They **will have to listen** carefully tomorrow.
4 • She is leaving in a minute. The **have to see** her right now.
5 • Our computer was broken. We **had to buy** another one.

EPISODE 25: Time to Go Home

EXERCISE 1	T	F
This episode is the last one.	X	
Marc and Lucie want to spend time with their friends and family.	X	
The blog received a lot of bad comments.		X
Marc took loads of pictures.	X	
Marc does not want to travel with Lucie anymore.		X
Marc forgot his suitcase at the hotel.	X	

EXERCISE 2

1 • What Lucie really loved was meeting all these people.
2 • People liked reading the blog to follow their adventures.
3 • Lucie was happy to share her paintings.
4 • One of the first things Marc wants to do is arrange all his pictures.
5 • At the end of the dialogue, it is time to check the luggage in.

EXERCISE 3

Lucie and Marc were very **happy** to write this blog and moved by readers' **positive** reactions. They are encouraging people to **travel**, even if the destination is close to their **home**. There is always **something** new to discover. They also want to keep on travelling and will certainly write more **posts** on their blog.

EXERCISE 4

1 • Marc and Lucie first visited African countries.
2 • Their blog contains texts, pictures and paintings.
3 • They really appreciated all the positive reactions about their blog.
4 • A new trip is one of Marc and Lucie's projects.
5 • They will certainly write their blog during their next trip.